Remembering What I Never
By Martin Hunt

To my dad. Sorry I didn't understand until far too late.

- Table of Contents

- **Contents**
- Chapter 1 Wilf   5
- Chapter 2   The Story of a Ride 18
- Chapter 3 Operation Pluto        77
- Chapter 4 V bombs       80
- Chapter 5 Operation Market Garden        85
- Chapter 6 The Battle of the Bulge        90
- Chapter 7  The Belsen Horror Camp.   100
- Chapter 8 Remembrance          112
- Chapter 9 Conclusion    116

Copyright © 2017 Martin Hunt
All Rights Reserved

**Chapter 1 Wilf**

My dad was just 18 years old when the Second World War stated. He was rejected by both the Navy and the Air Force on health grounds. Despite this, he served in the Army throughout the war. He became a driver in the Royal Army Service Corps. He often jested that he was turned down by the Air Force and the Navy because of his feet and ended up in the Infantry. I got the joke but could not make any sense of it until after his death. I was also puzzled when he laughingly called himself a "Desert Rat" as I had no doubt (and still don't) that he never served in Africa. I still do not really know what "flat feet" means, but it was clearly debilitating).
As a kid, I knew nothing of his wartime experiences. He would not talk about what he did in the war. He was always dismissive, saying he wasn't involved in any fighting. I learned very early that this was not a topic for discussion. Like most young boys, I was fascinated by the war. I was always drawing aircraft, mainly Lancasters, but others as well. I made Airfix models of planes and some ships. Strangely I had little interest in Army stuff, but I did have toy soldiers and played endlessly with them.
I recall some project in junior school where we had to build a model. I cannot remember the theme, but I could not think of anything to do. My mate, John Yates suggested a German concentration camp. I had never heard of them. I had no idea what they were, but for the lack of any idea, I agreed and we cobbled together a model, based upon nothing but imagination. I remember a sort of centre piece was a large, square one storey building (a factory, in my mind). It was painted in Imperial German colours of red, white and black and had a large Maltese cross on the roof. Thankfully, it had no swastikas and no resemblance whatsoever to reality.

I recall being really surprised and disappointed when the class teacher, Jack Bailey refused to show it on Parent's Evening. He just said it wasn't really a very nice thing to put on display. I had absolutely no idea why. I really loved Jack Bailey because he was a brilliant teacher. When I learned he had been a Mosquito pilot, my admiration was even greater. Jack also refused to discuss anything about the war and I just took it that no one would and no one liked being asked and it was not a thing to question.

I always admired my dad's war medals, but he was dismissive, saying none were for bravery, just for recognition of service and that everybody had them. I took it at face value and never enquired, but I always admired them because they were recognition of something. There was no internet in those days. Research was not possible, especially for a young schoolboy.

In my teens, I constantly asked questions, never about the war but even so, I found it hard to get my parents to talk to me about their families. We often visited family in Lincolnshire as both my parents were born there, (as were my brother and I). This thrilled me as it meant driving past loads of RAF stations. I was RAF mad. The ultimate joy was to pass RAF stations. Newton was an active RAF station, which was interesting enough, but I was always more thrilled to see the bigger stations that had been the base of Bomber Country in the second World War. Woodhall Spa and Waddington were awesome, but I was most impressed by Syerston. To a kid before his teens it was simply awesome.

The thin belt between Clifton in Nottingham to places like Newark, Sleaford and Wainfleet where various aunts, uncles and cousins lived made these stations regular sights of wonder and awe. I was always totally thrilled as we drove past. Occasionally, my dad would takes us miles out of the way, going northwards past Scampton. There was an Avro Lancaster standing proudly as a gate guardian. An actual, real Lancaster. It was the most awesome thing in my young life and I often badgered dad to take me to see it. I didn't know it was miles out of the way. I wouldn't have cared if I had and yet dad often indulged me and the sight of the thing never, ever diminished.

I can only imagine this was simply the indulgence of a son by a father. My dad was always dismissive of the RAF, calling them Brylcream boys. That muck was still universally used by all males in my youth and I still don't understand the insult. I was encouraged the smear the lard on my head as a kid, so I did not understand what was wrong with being a"Brylcream boy". I knew it was pejorative by his tone, but never pressed beyond the explanation that they were all "glory boys" and got all the women. There was always that tacit understanding never to ask. I knew enough to know that "getting all the women" was a grown-up problem and did not trouble myself with anything deeper.

Thus, I was always playing with soldiers or aircraft or warships and soaking up every tale I could glean about the war (I read the Victor every week and, whilst never talking about his personal experiences, my dad never discouraged me.

I left home to go to college in 1972. I visited regularly up until the death of my mum in 2014. At some point, during one of those visits, my dad gave a 6 page excerpt from his regimental company war diary to each of my brother, my sister and myself. He said "You've always wanted to know what I did in the war, so here it is."

This came from a recent holiday my parent's had taken on the Isle of Wight. I knew my dad adored the island and learned that he had served there during the war. I knew he had small reunions with former RASC colleagues whenever he visited the island and I came to believe that that was where he did his war service. The diary must have been given to him at his last mini reunion.

The pages were very poorly photocopied and had been very badly typed on a poor quality typewriter. On top of that, it was written in army jargon, which was pretty undecipherable. It mentioned place names that meant absolutely nothing to us. It used an army issue map of the time and without such a map, the map references were useless. Worse still, several places mentioned no longer exist (it never occurred to me that they could have been literally blown from existence). All of which made it very difficult to make any sense of it whatsoever. Stupidly, I assumed from his tone that was all he would give us, so I never pursued any questions with him. I simply did not think to ask, believing it was still taboo. Besides I lived over a hundred miles away from him and never got a great deal of time to get him to talk. After all, I knew virtually nothing about his brothers and sisters, let alone his war.

It is now ridiculous to me, but it never crossed my mind that he would talk. None of us could really understand the diary, so nothing really registered. My dad died in 2007 and it was when my brother and I were going through his papers that we found his army papers. It was a real shock that we then discovered that he had played a very active part in the liberation of Belsen. I recall being particularly shocked as I had formed a definite idea that he had spent his war service on the Isle of Wight and had never been to the front.

Both my brother and I have tried several routes to find more. My brother has visited Regimental Museums and I have corresponded with several with very little success. I have been scammed by web sites and struggled to find adequate sources. I am limited in that I cannot travel far. I found one book of interest was a single copy in the British Museum and I could only see it by personal visit, which is simply not possible. Other books have been hard to find and largely of little use. I have really struggled to find the answer to very basic questions, such as the number of lorries in a platoon, the logistics of the RASC, why his papers are marked TA when he served full time for over 5 years? How long was he on the Isle of Wight and where was he before?

His medals are indeed unimpressive in themselves. I thought the 1939-45 Star recognised his continuous war service throughout the war. He deserved a medal for that. Instead, I learn that one only had to serve 6 months during any of that time to qualify. I find this a horrible demeaning of the medal. Worse still his 1939-45 Defence Medal was available to virtually every Tom, Dick and Harry, you even qualified if you were in the YMCA! The 1939-45 War Medal was available to all who had served 28 days. Worst of all the France & Germany Medal was not restricted to those who served throughout 1944 to May 1945. Anyone who had spent one day in service in either of these countries qualified. My dad had nothing that showed that he was continuously in France, then Holland (as he always called it) and then Germany from August 1944 until sometime in 1946

I find this a gross diminishing of those medals, which utterly fails to recognise that his war service was heroic in its own way. Nevertheless, what I have learned is worth recording. Wilf was an ordinary bloke, working class, of peasant stock and minimal schooling. Even though he was an ordinary bloke and no special hero, a hero is exactly what he was. I know there were hundreds of thousands of others like him and they were doing the menial tasks rather than the actual fighting, but that fighting could not have been done without them and their service is completely overlooked and forgotten. As a member of that group, my dad deserves recognition for some remarkable service. His story should be told, even if it remains horribly sketchy.

In searching to make sense this, I found I was not alone. There are countless posts where people are trying to understand the war diaries of their fathers and grandfathers. Someone dies and then relatives are astounded to find that their dad/grandad was at Belsen and they ask how, why? What does this or that military designation mean? It is remarkable how many ask the same questions and also how none of them seem to be answered.

The problem starts with the fact that they were in the RASC. The Royal Army Service Corps was responsible for all the logistics of supplying and transporting troops and their munitions. That is a huge operation and includes all the administration of logistics, not just the actual transportation of it. It also includes driving all the Ambulances and non-combatant vehicles, staff cars, despatch riders etc.

This was not done from a central RASC base. Each unit absorbed RASC men for such tasks. Thus my dad was with 2 Coy, RASC on his pay-book. In fact he was assigned to units as required and became a member of that unit until reassigned. After landing in Normandy, he effectively became part of the XXX Corps, more specifically, the 50th (Northumbrian) Division. He was not a Geordie; he had not fought with that unit in Africa but he became one of them for about a year. None of that is overt to people seeking someone who was in the RASC.

This search (like many others) came from the surprise of reading a company war diary. My dad's certainly made no sense on first reading. I have learned that the company diary is not that helpful. There is no detail of their journeys in terms of distance, cargo etc. There is no context of the wider battles going-on. In fact the diary is effectively mainly about the travels of the company HQ, which was usually well behind the platoons doing the actual job and so doesn't even tell the real story.

There is no explanation of how many men nor how many vehicles in a platoon. It assumes all of these are obvious, but 70 years on, the army is a very different beast. The RASC disappeared in 1965 and its identity has changed more since then. There is no record that I could find explaining the organization structure of those times. How many platoons in a company? How many men in a platoon? How many vehicles in a platoon?; How many men to a lorry?

Once a company joins another unit, it could become an Ambulance, supply vehicle, fuel bowser or infantry carrier for an artillery unit or a tank transporter (amongst many other things). Each would have different structure and platoon, company sizes etc. All of which is utterly lost in the narrow references of an RASC company diary which is very much focused upon the company HQ. For obvious reasons, the diary does not give the bigger picture. It does not give any context (nor detail) to the entries. Although this diary ends before they were sent to relieve Belsen, there is no mention of the Battle of the Falaise pocket, the Battle of Antwerp, Operation Market Garden, and the Battle of the Bulge (although it does once refer to the "Von Rundstedt push" in the midst of the most chaotic part of the entire diary) despite being actively involved in all of these.

Any references to chains of command are now very hard to understand. They get assigned to this command or that command and 70 years on, their simple numbers mean nothing to the average reader. Map references are to maps which no longer exist. Orders to move are ignorant of the bigger picture. Communications at this time were very basic. There were no radio sets on lorries, no mobile phones, no "satnav". The only way communicating with platoons is by physically catching up with them. Thus the company diary inevitably refers to the difficulties and experience of the company HQ, which is invariably well behind the platoons which are with their allocated units chasing the Germans as quickly as possible.

There is a touching letter from the people of Aalst, thanking the company for a surprise Christmas party they arranged for the children of Aalst. You have to dig elsewhere to put that in context. The dreadful privations on the people of Holland are now little known outside of the Netherlands. Thousands were effectively starved to death by the Nazi attrition. The Dutch Resistance had been rendered unusable by German infiltration of the movement. That is little known. The suggestion that Operation Market Garden itself was betrayed by a turned resistance member is generally ignored. In fact,

It is not understood that the threat of V1 and V2 weapons was far greater in the Netherlands than anywhere else. Finding their launch sites and putting them out of commission was a massive part of this charge through the low-countries and is little understood now. However, V2 were the world's first SCUDs. Their launch sites were mobile and therefore so much harder to find, let alone put out of action. I recall how little success our special forces had in locating them during the Gulf Wars years later and with spy satellite technology. In 1944 there was, no such technologies and no precedent to learn from. I recall that David Niven was pootling about on such a task on behalf of "the Phantom Regiment" which was later called the SAS and they've being doing this sort of thing ever since. But then, it was fast and unknown and very scary. Much scarier than Blair telling us years later that Saddam's Scuds could hit us in 45 minutes. Sadly, back then, it was actually very real except a V2 took only 4 minutes to soundlessly find its target.

Despite concerted efforts, I remain frustrated at the difficulty in making sense of the diary. It is frightening how much of our history is fading from memory. It is even more frightening as the level of ignorance grows and perceptions get distorted. So much of this diary takes so much for granted. It assumes (probably correctly) that its entries make sense to the reader at that time. Sadly it fails to give understanding to the reader 70 years after the event. I would encourage people to dig into it more. These things need to be put in context and made relevant. I fear the acquired ignorance is driving us to the frightening possibility of history repeating itself. The tendency to make scapegoats and spread fear and mistrust is ever-growing. It seems we need to remind ourselves how easily fascism can grow and the evil extremes that mankind can be driven to by little more than suggestion.

## Chapter 2   The Story of a Ride

(From the War Diary of 20 Company, Royal Army Service Corps)

The following is reproduced from 6 pages which were poorly reproduced and difficult to follow. The entry for each date is verbatim. All emphases are as per the original, as are all errors. In order to try and make sense of the entries, a comment has been added after each verbatim copy of the original text. Wherever possible, the location has been identified in context of the journey, attempting to give a distance and direction of travel. Attempts have been made to translate as much jargon as possible, but the broader context of Brigades and Divisions has proved ridiculously unattainable. Where key operations are involved, an initial attempt to give some background has been made. There is nothing here that would not benefit from considerably more research. Research is extremely difficult as records are poor. It may need a visit to the British Library as at least one reference book is unique to that institution. There is no other copy available.

The original 6 pages, where so much was simply assumed to be understandable is now very difficult to understand and therefore to follow. 70 years after the fact, much of the jargon had become unfathomable. I am therefore attempting to make sense the context and keep the story in people's minds. It is startling to see how little people remember despite commemorating Remembrance Day every year. There is little perception of the hardship and danger faced by those who were not in the front line. I am sure that this is due to perceptions from the First World War, that if you were not at the front, you were safe from all enemy action.

No thought at all is given to the reality. Those troops at the very front were wholly dependent upon people like my dad. Not only in being transported (they were literally chasing the enemy constantly and needed to be driven as quickly as possible to wherever they needed to be. They were totally dependent on these drivers for ammunition, petrol and basic supplies. The drivers had to stay permanently close enough to the fighting troops to keep them supplied as they raced into Germany on the heels of a very fierce enemy. Not a thought is given to the fact that none of these drivers were "fit for active service". Technically, they were all deemed fit only for home service and yet they were close to the front throughout the last year of the Reich and did indeed actually have to actually fight the enemy at times.

This story is worth telling in itself, as testimony to the contribution made by such men. It does not touch upon the ultimate horror as it ends in March 31st (my dad's birthday) 1945. It tells nothing of how, three weeks later they were heavily involved in the greatest horror of all when they were active in the relief of the Belsen-Bergen "horror camp". Even that hideous event is now largely misunderstood and learning some truths have shown how necessary it is to record something about it all in honour of all those ordinary blokes who "did their bit" a lot more than was ever appreciated.

Aug 1st 1944- March 31st 1945

**August 1st** "Weather Showery. Fine intervals. Location WEYBRIDGE. Vehicles in need of much maintenance having stood loaded with three tons of ammn. each and water-proofed for 46 consecutive days."

Comment: This opening begs lots of questions. Why Weybridge? Weybridge is within the modern M25, West South West of inner London. It is known that the company had been involved in Operation PLUTO on the Isle of Wight. Most of the D-Day concentrations of troops and equipment had been based in the South West, Cornwall and Devon in particular. PLUTO was initially trialled between IoW and the South West, (Swansea and Bristol being terminals for the oil pipe which was laid to fuel the invasion. It seems odd therefore that the company is now in the South East, close to London and had been waiting, fully-loaded, there for 46 days, since the 22$^{nd}$ June (16 days after the invasion landings). Whilst it is understandable having the stored ammunition well away from the embarkation camps, Weybridge still seems rather close to London, with the first V1 hitting England on June 13$^{th}$ and the South East (especially London) being the prime target. However, it is known that other RASC units, carrying fuel, food and other supplies were transported from Tilbury docks just after D-Day and had to sail from the Thames, round the South East coast before they reached the setting off point for Normandy (on the South West coast, around Portsmouth and the Solent area.

All lorries had to be waterproofed to a standard approved by REME Inspections prior to transfer to LSTs (Landing Ship, Tank) and that the time waiting was 46 days, not the period of continuous waterproofing.

**August 2$^{nd}$** "Information received Coy. Will assist in move of 21 Army Gp rear overseas."

Comment: Being unaware of the context, other than in terms of much wider history, it has to be inferred that the rear group is about to be despatched to reinforce the forward part of 21st Army group who had been fighting in France from the landings on 6th June, without a break. There is no indication where the 21 Army Group (rear) are located, but as the 20th Company's lorries are already loaded with ammunition, it seems fair to assume that they would carry this ammunition in support of the Army group, rather than transport the actual troops to the embarkation point. I have since learned that the RASC had 3 basic types of load, troops, petrol and ammunition (I suspect that food and other supplies were mixed with the troop and perhaps the ammunition transports. The latter two were always kept separate for fear of petrol fires igniting ammunition. However, ammunition was relatively safe to transport and 20th Company were certainly appear to have been carrying ammunition at this point.

**August 10th** "Movement order received. All TCV in A.Gp. area H.Q. and Workshops in assembly area. O.C. to lead whole column to Marshalling Area at 6.0am following day"

Comment: It is hard to translate with certainty. TCV refers to Troop Carrying Vehicle. These appear to have been dispersed, but have now been assembled together (presumably at a camp in Weybridge) and the necessary Head Quarters (presumably of the RASC) and the workshops for vehicle maintenance have been established within the assembly area. The Officer Commanding (OC) of the RASC (no indication of strength, only that 20th Company is amongst them) is then to lead the whole column (no indication of size nor of constituent parts) to the Marshalling area on the next morning. It seems plausible to assume that the RASC has joined the 21st Army Group (rear) and will lead the column (presumably, the troops will follow to the Marshalling area). There is no indication as to the location of this assembly point. One is led to infer that it is still Weybridge. Neither is it clear as to whether there are TCV's extra to the ones full of ammunition. Whichever the case, 8 days have gone unrecorded, during which time, either the ammunition was transported and unloaded somewhere else, or else new TCVs arrived. It is also possible that the whole company and the ammunition have moved to an unknown assembly point during those 8 days. Given the need for secrecy at the time, this is highly plausible, but it makes interpretation 70 years later very subjective.

**August 11th** "Arrived Marshalling Area. Convoy not loaded in accordance with craft loads. Splitting of loads commenced and continued all through the night."
Not being aware of craft loads, it would seem that the lorries arrived at the marshalling Area (presumably very close to the embarkation point) and then had to be re-arranged in terms of weight distribution in order to be driven onto the LSTs without difficulty. It may be that factors affecting the necessary rearrangements could include; Putting each company of soldiers and their ammunition trucks in an order that would ensure safe, rapid loading of the LSTs and in correct order for disembarkation, so there would be no need for rearrangement after landing in France (which may have been a little more precarious).

**August 12th** " Convoy proceeds to embarkation point (GOSPORT) with completely bogus Nominal Roll and arrives 6.30 am. 7.30 am loading on to L.S.T. commenced. Owing to inaccuracy tables, two TCV left on bank. L.S.T. convoy complete and leaguered in Cowes Roads 5.0 pm."

Note: Gosport is a 70 mile drive south west from Weybridge, but there is no indication as to the location of the Marshalling area . It seems odd to identify the point of origin and the point of embarkation, but nothing in between. It seems odd that an official diary uses am and pm (in varying formats, (e.g. a.m. or am) instead of the usual military format of the 24 hour clock.

Comment: It is unclear as to whom was responsible for the miscalculated loading tables, but it seems fair to assume that these were drawn up by general staff of the D-day planners and had nothing to do with either the LST crews nor their passengers. It is also intriguing to know what happened to the two vehicles left behind (were the men left with them, did they catch a later transport? etc.). "Leaguer" is a noun for the encampment of a besieging army. "Cowos Roads" has no clear explanation. One inference is that it is a code-name used by the planners, perhaps indicating lines of LSTs awaiting orders to sail.

**August 13th** "Part of convoy reaches ARROMANCHES. Three L>S>T> put back to port with varying troubles including ship with O.C. aboard."

Comment: Arromanches-aux-bains is a small port, (close to the town of Bayeux where they have a reputation for sewing). It is roughly half way between the British Gold beach and the infamous Omaha beach. The Gold priority was to capture Arromanches and then link up with the Americans from Omaha beach. Arromanches was key in order to allow supplies and troops from England to reinforce the invaders. It was captured on 7th June. Bayeaux soon followed, but linking with the Americans was impeded by the nightmare landings of Omaha beach. Arromanches was where the famous Mulberry harbours were towed 2 days later and it was here that the convoy landed. On 19th June, Mulberry A (at Omaha beach) had been destroyed by storms, thus the only way into France at the time was at Arromanches until Antwerp was taken 6 months later, the Mulberry Harbour there became known as Port Winston. Infuriatingly, there is no quantity given for how big or small a part of the company actually disembarked in France initially. We know 3 LSTs turned back to Gosport, but not what proportion of the company were on those LSTs

**August 15th** "Balance of Company, less two TCV reaches Arromanches and Coy concentrate in Bayeux area. Maintenance."

Comment; There is no indication as to what caused the delays nor what happened in the interval. Presumably, those that landed would not be allowed to wait near Port Winston as they would have blocked the flow of traffic. They must have been in Arromanches town, near the Mulberry. Again, there is no indication in terms of vehicles, troop numbers or cargo as to the size of the company, nor (apart from the lorries) how much was lost by those two original vehicles being unable to embark in the first place. It is, however, clear that they have not caught up with their unit, despite 3 LSTs returning with part of the company and a whole intervening (unmentioned) day.

**August 16th** "Coy to come under command 5 L. of C. Sub area. Stand-by instructions received for hospital details. Coy advised no details for a few days and maintenance to continue. 11.15 pm – Urgent message received. Coy to move immediately to COULVAIN and come under command CRASC 50 (Northumberland) Division. Whole unit moved 1.30 am 17

Comment: L. of C. is army abbreviation for "line of communication". The detail of 5 L of C sub area is not digitised and can be obtained from the National Archive (at a cost) in paper form only. It does not seem worthwhile here, as it has but a fleeting relevance to this story. CRASC possibly means commander RASC, in charge of the transport convoy, attached to the 50th Northumberlands. Military interpretation is required here for accuracy. Maintenance was the process of maintaining all supplies, effectively, driving a delivery shuttle. Coulvain is 22 miles south of Bayeux, it is reach via Villers-Bocage, a small village about 2 miles east of Coulvain. Villers Bocage was the scene of one of the fiercest battles immediately after D-Day, it was taken on 14th June and the 50th Northumberlands were an essential part of the battle and subsequent occupation. It could be inferred that the 20th Company set off at 1.30 on the morning of 17th; however, given the "urgency" it is more likely that the whole company was roused, assembled and driven at speed to arrive 2 hours and 15 minutes after the order was received.

**August 18th** "TCVs carrying 69 and 231 Brigades push on through Proussy. HQ leaguer in PROUSSY among unburied dead and stinking cows."

Comment: Proussy is 19 miles south east of Coulvain and is the place where Montgomery made his tactical Head Quarters in August 1944. The convoy has almost caught up with the front line. It is odd that the stinking cows seem to cause more offence than the unburied dead, who would also have been stinking by then. Perhaps it indicates that the diarist is new to the scene of unburied corpses and blames the smell upon the more familiar or least unusual. Military knowledge is required to estimate the size of 69 and 231 Brigades and therefore of the convoy.

**August 19th** "Push continues through CONDE sur NOIVREAU (Badly damaged) with H.Q. bivouacing at FLERS MR 7F/883371. Burial of dead far from complete due excessive numbers (the Germans lost. Rain."
Comment: Conde sur Noivreau is 3 miles south West of Proussy and Flers a further 8 miles south. The map reference given depends upon having the map issued to the RASC at the time. Conde is on the north east edge of the Falaise pocket (which was at Argentan, about 20 miles to the east of the town), where the Germans were encircled. The battle lasted from 12th -21st August, so it was still on-going when they arrived. They are at the front (or within 20 miles of it). Effectively, they have caught up with the troops that have fought their way here from the D-Day landings. In fact, the British had been tied up around Caen since D-Day. It was the intense fighting here that gave the Americans much less opposition to the East allowing the break out. The Germans lost 800,000 men in the battle, comprising 240,000 dead or wounded and the remainder taken prisoner (who would not have been moved by trucks, but would have had to have been supplied by them once they had been taken prisoner). The allies lost 37,000 ground forces killed and 210,000 injured in the battle. The Allies also lost 17,000 airmen over Normandy between June 6th and August 21st.

**August 20th** "Push continued. Contact Platoons. No casualties, many prisoners. H.Q. move to ATHIS with plns now well ahead."

Comment: This needs further research as it has been impossible so far to find an Athis between Flers and Argentan (a future destination, 37 miles east of Flers). There is an Athis near Mons, but that is too far east (over 200 miles) and the Germans had a grass strip aerodrome there which was not attacked until 22$^{nd}$ August (by US fighter planes) and must therefore have been far too close to the enemy for any allied HQ at that time, (although they were definitely headed in that direction). The "contact with platoons" refers effectively to reaching the front lines, but there is no indication as to which platoons, nor how many, nor to the proximity of the enemy. The phrase; "plns now well ahead" must be relative to the new HQ position and not the column (which has caught up with the Platoons). It has to be remembered that these lorries did not carry radios. It would be impossible to communicate with them whilst they were mobile or elsewhere.

**August 21$^{st}$** "Coy H.Q. lagging behind due to road congestion and out of touch with Plns. Leaguered night MIQUILLAUME. Heavy rain. Rum issue – Cheers!"

Comment: Again, it has not been possible at first attempt to locate Miquillaume. There is no indication of the cause of congestion. It could be troop/supply movement and/or refugees. There is a high death rate of French civilians during the fighting, Conde sur Noivreau had been badly damaged and thus a flow of refugees seems very likely. It seems odd that the (much larger) column has advanced through these barriers, but reference is only made to explain the delay of the (slower advance) of the HQ. Again, the entry refers to the HQ (which was "lagging behind" rather than the current position of the column. The rum ration was clearly necessary to raise spirits of the column as the push is clearly very slow and difficult. Perhaps it was issued to all because the battle of the Failaise pocket had ended.

**August 22$^{nd}$** "Into ARGENTAN – still long way behind PLNs. Arrived midnight."

Comment: Argentans is only about 20 miles east of Flers and it has taken at least 3 and possibly 4 days to get there(it does not stipulate whether they arrived at midnight on 22st or 23rd). An average of 10 – 13 miles a day by lorry for 3 or 4 days shows how hard progress was.

**August 23rd** "Contact made with Plns. No casualties though well forward and in range of enemy constantly and in among enemy pockets left behind in the advance. H.Q. holdup for hours outskirts of CHAMBOIS among stinking dead horses and both Allied and enemy dead. Masses of abandoned equipment littering roads. Distance of 24 miles took 7 hours to cover."

NB PLNS presumably refers to the Platoons of the column which form the 20th company RASC. There is no record of the experience of these platoons in their earlier (than the HQ) journey "No casualties" refers to 20th Company RASC, not the entire convoy, but they have reached the front. Neither does it mention the troops they were originally carrying. It is unconceivable that they would still be riding on the lorries and passing platoons that had been fighting at the front for weeks. It is unclear what is on the lorries, but very clear how much their load is needed.

Comment: The diary entry is fairly clear about the state of things at the front. Chambois is about 8 miles east then 3 miles north from Argentans. There is no indication of time of arrival, nor of final destination. It is odd that it emphasises the difficult going as 24 miles in 7 hours seems very fast compared to the previous 4 days. It is probably due to encountering the enemy, the sudden threat of being in range of the enemy and the number of corpses around them all being more immediate than the previous reference to bodies that were encountered longer after the action had ended in that area. The debris of equipment around the road would also have been a shocking encounter, but was only mentioned as a reason for the HQ falling behind, without explaining how the column had negotiated it more successfully (August 20th). As there was a major and massive battle going within 10 miles of the column at the time, the Company diary entry is remarkably understated.

**August 24th** "H.Q. moved 5.50 am with view catch up with plns. Laigle area. Due route road congestion did not arrive before mid-night. Contact made with Plns. No casualties but personnel unable to sleep in vehicles – sadly in need of tentage or like cover, Sick states nil, despite foul weather and lack of decent rest.
Comment: L'Aigle is approximately 30 miles east of Chambois and the H.Q is trying to move to that area. Whatever destination was reached in the L'Aigle area (clearly not the town itself) took over 18 hours, but the distance can only be put at around 25miles. At least this has put the HQ in contact with the platoons. There is never any reference reported from the platoons about their earlier experiences of the journey, only of the HQ staff. However the casualty and sickness reports refer to the whole company (including the platoons). The remarks about difficult conditions and lack of adequate supplies (e.g. tents) clearly show the difficulties which account for the lack of sleep. I suspect the tentage problem is for the troops being carried rather than just drivers. It is unfortunate that there is no reference to the mileage made over any period of time, nor length of periods between rests to actually show how tough conditions have been.
**August 25th** "Whole Coy on maintenance and rest. The first since Aug 16th. Much needed sleep obtained."
Comment: The reference clearly shows some welcome respite, but does not quantify how much maintenance was required, not indeed as to how much rest was achieved. One can only assume that the maintenance was light and the rest and sleep were equally divided amongst the whole company. Maintenance does not mean time-off; it means routine deliveries to maintain supplies at the front.
**August 27th** "H.Q. through to MISERY ("76671) after journey of only 7 miles throughout the whole of 26th. Plns further forward and contacted in the MANTES area. No casualties8.30 pm Plns to return to H.Q. area and stand by for maintenance lift".

Comment: Despite being just 7 miles from where ever the H.Q. was in the L'Aigle area, it has not been possible to locate, hence there is no clear idea of distance, nor route taken. Nor is there an explanation as to how the Platoons are in the Mantes area, which is 70 miles away, roughly East North East of L'Aigle. Mantes is on the Seine and on the outskirts of Paris (which is 30 miles West South West of Mantes). Mantes is the place where General Patton crossed the Seine on August 24th in his famous race to Paris. How the Platoons can be 10 times further ahead of HQ who could only go 7 miles in over 24 hours is unexplained. Nor is it clear why the Platoons had to drive all the way back to HQ rather than meet somewhere in between. What is clear is that the allies are literally chasing the Germans across the Seine. The need to press forward as fast as possible needs the maintenance lift to get as many troops forward as possible (in an attempt to overtake the German retreat) and to keep them all fully supplied.

**August 28th** "O.C. complains to CRASC unfair flog drivers to such extent, having regards fact Dvrs are required fresh for immediate troop lifts. CRASC explains situation vital and maintenance flogs essential and exhorts all to stick it out.10.0 am. CRASC 2 Tank Tptr Coln contacts HQ and says unit is under command. CRASC 30 Corp contacts HQ hour later says unit is under command. Both formations want returns. Latter details Coy to move. CRASC 50 (N) Div cancels all foregoing. Coy to stay with him. 11.45 pm TCVs from ROUGLES flog not yet in though due for repeat flog at 5.0 am. O.C. again contacts CRASC pointing out weariness of Drvs and also some grief amongst vehicles, and some vehicles missing."

Comment: This clearly gives a taste of how things are rather fraught. It is clear that men and machines have been pushed to the limit and they are getting close to breaking point. A "flog" is clearly a phrase indicating a flat-out drive to a location. The reference to CRASC 2 Tank Tptr Coln is as yet undeciphered. Clearly a Tank Transporter is involved, but I can offer no sense to the use of Coln as a qualifier. Where the CRASC 2 is located, nor to whom he is "under command" is not known, neither is it clear to whom 30 Corp are "under command". It seems both are held at the location of their deliverery and are asking for orders to return to HQ (thus releasing them from being "under command" of the Officer–in-charge of their delivery point). 50 (N) Div refers to the 50th Northumberlands that were picked up earlier, but I have no idea what is meant by "all foregoing". Rugles ("ROUGLES") is half way between Flers and Paris.

**August 29th** "1.10 am TCVs contacted in traffic jams up and down drag, and Pln Officers advised they must turn round on delivery of loads and proceed for further loads. OC returns HQ location to receive message that detail is cancelled. Sets out again in endeavour make fresh contact Pln Officers and stop turn round. All TCV hold at FMC. Report Centre by 8.0 am. CRASC Instructs unit will accept no orders whatsoever except as issued by him. All TCVs now to be collected in HQ area and proceed of troop lift of 231 and 69 Bdes at 10.0 am. Plns out with Bdes by mid-day. CRASC Conference 5.0 pm says Bdes will cross SEINE possibly tonight. Heavy rain and a dam' awful night for all concerned."

Comment: It seems that lorries and crews are effectively being requisitioned wherever they deliver a load. Whilst handy for those at the front to gain more mobility, it would soon cripple the push if no supplies were possible because all lorries had effectively been diverted to local needs. Thus the need to prevent this forces the order to ignore all orders except from their own regimental O.C. was reinforced by actually driving to and fro along the route and passing this order directly to each Platoon Commander. After all this effort to maintain the to and fro of supplies delivery, the orders change again and all vehicles have to report back to HQ to collect the troops and get them rapidly across the Seine. The stress of the uncertainty, changing plans and constant urgency are clearly telling. 69 Brigade was a 2$^{nd}$ line TA unit which had been part of the 23$^{rd}$ (Northumbrian) Division which had to be disbanded because of its heavy losses over the past 2 months. The Brigade had only just been newly absorbed into the 50$^{th}$ (Northumbrian) Division. There are clear signs of communication breakdown and confusion, probably to do with the loss of a whole Division. One can therefore understand the confusion at the time and can only imagine the stress behind it. These troops must have been quite traumatised at that time.

**August 30$^{th}$** "HQ crossed Seine on pontoon well behind Plns a few minutes before midnight after being held less than one mile from location for best part of day. Arrived TILLY 2.0. am and leagured. Rain continued. Pontoon across SEINE 750 feet long put across under fire only short while before PLNS crossed in less than 15 hours"
Comment: The final sentence makes no sense. The most likely interpretation is that earlier in the day, the Platoons had crossed in under 15 hours, whilst hours later, the 250 yard crossing under fire was much more hazardous. The fact that they were virtually held all day, less than a mile from the crossing point shows how heavy the bottleneck at the pontoon had become.

**August 31st** "Contact made with Plns in AMIENS area, then standing by proceed to ARRAS and thence if all goes well, BRUSSELS. No casualties, but vehicles badly needing maintenance or Workshops attention. HQ to CUIGNY and no further."

Amiens is 100 miles North North East from the Seine crossing. Arras is a further 65 miles North East of Arras and Brussels another hundred miles East North East of Arras. There is no sign of Cuigny on modern maps. All we know is that it is on the N25 between Amiens and Arras and it is much closer to the former than the latter. Despite the planned objectives being stated, the actual mileage achieved is still extremely small. After a 100 mile push with little resistance as far as Amiens, they are really struggling to get further to Arras.

**1944.**

**Sept. 1** "Fruitless attempt made by O.C. contact Plns. CRASC confirms Div intention is to head for BRUSSELS just as hard as they can go."

Comment: There is no explanation as to why the HQ following behind the rapidly advancing platoons continuously makes much slower progress; HQ itself does not know exactly where the platoons are. One would assume that CRASC is with HQ rather than the Platoons and that the order is effectively that they should not slowdown in order for HQ to catch up.

**September 2nd** "Platoons through to ALBERT and ARRAS and in among fighting. C Pln with Lt. Brooks take prisoners on their own. B Pln successfully engage and withdraw from enemy ambush, all while leaguering awaiting pick up infantry. 4.0. pm TCVs stand by to go forward with Guards Bde to BRUSSELS, 120 miles ahead"

**Comment:**

It would seem the N25 was impassable due to enemy defence. Instead they reach Amiens via Albert which is on the road to Cambrai and is only 16 miles East North East of Amiens. Even there, they encounter enemy action, albeit lighter and manageable. It should be noted that the RASC was responsible for its own defence/protection and hence the recording of action is by the Platoons themselves and not the troops they were carrying. It is interesting to note that this is the first time where destination and distance are given together, thus giving an indication of direction for the first time since Weybridge. My dad was in B platoon. Here is absolute proof that he took part in actual front-line fighting. His platoon were ambushed and had to fight their way out. RASC members were trained to fight as infantry and were responsible for their own defence. Something he always kept from his children, despite giving us a copy of this diary towards the end of his life.

**September 3rd** "O.C. contacts Plns en route to BRUSSELS in LENS. No casualties. Vehicles in some instances just carrying loads and no more. HQ standing by in DOULLENS area for move forward. Colossal welcome from civilian population to troops of the B.L.A. O.C. returns to Coy location to find all other units gone. 2nd i/c no information or instructions for move. O.C, directs HQ will move forthwith. Convoy moves off 11.45 pm."

Comment: The Platoons are in Lens, 12 miles north of Arras, whilst the HQ is 40 miles behind in Doullens ( which is 19miles North of Amiens and 27 miles South West of Arras).I believe BLA is the British Army of Liberation. The area they are in is essentially the Somme and virtually everywhere is famous for the horrors of World War 1.

**September 4th** "HQ arrives RAIN CHEVAL 2.0. am and pushes into unoccupied Chateau adjoining a V.1. site Chateau only just vacated by personnel of enemy HQ. Rooms filled with useful loot sealed off and Police advised. Capt. Hyde with last remaining spare TCV leaves for BRUSSELS to catch up with Plns. HQ prepares move to LENS. O.C. meets CRASC 2 Tank Tptr. a.m.who has 6 of this unit's vehicles with him and which went on detachment in England. Immediate request for their return made on the spot. Sgt. Brooks shoots himself in the foot in a civilian melee welcoming unit HQ into LENS. Plns through to ANTWERP area and meeting with heaviest resistance so far met. L/Cpl Davey killed when running into a string of mines which were being laid against possible enemy counter-attacks. Dvr. Chilcott badly wounded. A Platoon mortared and shelled in location. No (other) casualties. Company mourns loss of Davey – a good soldier, killed in execution of a dangerous duty."

Comment: The reference of occupying a chateau full of loot, freshly vacated by fleeing Germans brings home how close to the front the column is. The reference to a V.1 site is chilling (the RAF had been systematically bombing these since late 1943, but many were still active and very deadly. It should be noted that Antwerp was not taken for a further two months of fierce fighting as it was the vital deep water port that the Allies needed to get a secure and bigger landing of troops and supplies for the push into Germany. 2,500 V1 (world's first cruise missile –called the "doodlebug") were fired at Antwerp during the struggle for the port. The confusion of command is demonstrated by catching the CRASC 2 having "commandeered" company trucks to accompany his Tank Transporters. The reference to Sgt. Brooks seems comic, especially in relation to the subsequent recording of dead and wounded. However, being shot in the foot really is not funny. The loss of L/Cpl Davey to "friendly fire" shows the perils of the job being far more than just being shot at, shelled and mortared. In September 1944 it was decided to bombard Antwerp with V2 rockets. More V2s were fired on Antwerp than were fired at London, yet this is not widely understood now. From October 1944 till march 1945 5960 rockets (v1 and v2) were launched at Antwerp.

**September 5th** "HQ in AVION. B.Pln ambushed with Devons and Dorsets in TOURNAI area. Pln Bren teams did good work in helping extricate all personnel without casualties. Pln credited with killing fair bag of enemy attempting de-bus. Brigade express appreciation our Drivers of their willingness to get out and want to fight despite responsibilities of vehicles, and wearying long hours at wheel."

Comment: Avion is 2 miles south of Lens. Tournai is about 38 miles West North West of Lens and is a few miles over the border in Belgium. The Devon and Dorsets were supporting the Guards Armoured brigade. My dad's platoon is not only in the midst of the action, it is acquitting itself very well. The commendation to the drivers (my dad was one of them) shows how committed they were, despite the stress of being over worked and suffering punishing lack of sleep as well as the stress of being under constant threat, even during times when not actually under attack . It should be remembered that none of these men were graded as medically fit for action abroad.

**September 6th** " HQ move into TOURNAI …" (rest of entry lost)

**September 8th** "Plns in Antwerp filling their boots but being continually sniped. O.C. sends message to Pln Comdrs that looting is a serious offence. C Pln go forward with 69 Bde over new canal crossing to North. Vehicle situation to date: 4TCV knocked out; 1 TCV burned out; 2 TCV evacuated due to crashes; 1 TCV lost without trace – (Pinched?)

Personnel situation: 1 killed, 1 wounded, 1 missing (Dr Graves' last seen stung in the mouth by a wasp and running round in ever increasing circles.)"

Comment: There is a clear sense of relief in this entry. Despite the fact that its troops are looting Antwerp, there seems to be a sense of "turning a blind eye", accepting the inevitable, timeless result of warfare. It seriously understates the situation though. Although Brussels and Antwerp had been captured by the British, the Scheldt estuary remained in German hands and the German garrison were fiercely defending the access to the port. Antwerp was not opened as a port until late November. Weeks after this entry, the Battle of the Scheldt lasted five weeks and cost over 12,000 Allied dead half of them Canadian who led the attack , which lasted over 5 weeks. Thus, Antwerp remained a very dangerous place. The reference to Driver Graves is funny (not for him, but compared to the other possibilities, it is light relief).

**September 9th** "H.Q. moved to ZOERTS PARWYS (Sh. 3. BL 9981). Cpl Wylie with Dorsets highly commended by C.O. for personal gallantry in working on blazing Bren Carrier loaded with ammn. Until ordered to desist. Subsequent explosion killed 3 wounded 4. Cpl Wylie recommended for mention in despatches."

Comment: Zoerles-Parwys is 22 east south east of Antwerp. Despite no mention of the proximity to the enemy, the reference to Corporal Wylie's action show by implication that the area is dangerous and under enemy fire. There is no mention of whether or not the mention in despatches was authorised (only that it was recommended). The severity of the risk and the outcome again shows that the Platoons were in the midst of serious action and their lives were at serious risk.

**September 10th** "Contact with Plns by O.C. No casualties and day's maintenance in hand."

**September 12th** "H.Q. moved to DIEST area mid-day. O.C. interview wirh Brigdr Comdg 231 Bde, who states he is extremely satisfied with work of troop carrying personnel. O.C. subsequently contacts Pln Officers and tells them with a bit more attention could be considered doing reasonable job of work. Pln o's very grateful for such high praise. Slight night-time shelling of Pln areas. No casualties, though some damage to superstructure of TCV's."

Comment: Diest is 15 miles South East of Zoerles-Parijs. There is a humorous insight into the "stiff upper lip" approach of the military, from the O.C. under-playing his message to officers to their reception of it as high praise. Something wonderfully British about understatement. Again, understating that they were constantly shelled throughout the night, with sufficient closeness to cause damage to lorries is wonderfully understated, almost funny in the nonchalance with which it is reported.

**September 13th** "CRASC 50, (N) Div instructs O.C. to go out of command and come under Cmd 2nd Army in HALS (South of Brussels) Coy to concentrate and move rearwards forthwith. Conc. Completed along MAIDERT-ZEEHLAM road by 9.0 pm and move commenced. Canal bridgehead bombed as tail of convoy cleared area. Whole Coy moves through the night."

Comment: It has been impossible to locate Hals, Maldert or Zeehlam, so the entry is very confusing. Nevertheless, Hals is clearly south of Brussels which is only 40 miles west of Diest (and clearly in a rearwards direction). It is most likely Frans Hals Square, which is in the municipality of Anderlecht, some 10 miles south east of central Brussels. The issue of concentration involves bringing all the vehicles together from their disparate locations; this takes most of the day, so lorries are presumably returning from some distance away from the assembly point. They only just escape as the canal bridgehead is bombed just after the last vehicle has got across.

**September 14th** " Move completed and Coy in NOSSINGEM by 3.0 am. O.C. reports to 2nd army 9.0 am and informed Coy not wanted, and to return to previous location. O.C. keeps temper. Thousands of vehicle miles utterly wasted, but personnel take opportunity for look around BRUSSELS, while unit rep. reports to CRASC 50 Div, with 2nd Army instructions. Coy instructed to report to CRASC 30 Corps Troops on BOOM-ANTWERP road earliest. Plns in new area in Botanical Gardens (Not in Zoo) by 9.30pm and standing by for supply detail. O.C. still keeps temper, but with difficulty."

Comment: Nossingem, does not exist. It is most likely Nossegem, which is about 12 miles east of central Brussels (and about 40 west miles from Diest). Thus the to and fro from Diest is about 100 miles. To account for "thousands of vehicle miles" puts the number of vehicles in the tens, but without a clue as to how many thousands, it is still impossible to hazard a guess as to how many TCVs form a company. It is worth noting that the Botanical Gardens are not in the Zoo. The escape of dangerous animals from wartime zoos did cost lives. The chance of some R&R, exploring Brussels was an unexpected breather and clearly very welcome.

**September 16th** "Coy proceeds to BOURG LEOPOLD for troop carrying duties. Traffic congestion causes long delays en route. Coy generally "mucked about".

Comment: The wasted journeys, the uncertainty of command and of orders have certainly affected morale. Previous (and more severe) road blockages did not affect morale. The comment "mucked about" is a sign of frustration, having driven extremely hard and seen action and been praised, there is a sense of feeling unappreciated, confused and angry in that mildly worded entry. In fact, the trucks had advanced beyond their fuel capacity and were dependent upon other trucks bringing them fuel from Arromanches. Antwerp was not open due to the Germans holding the estuary. Pluto could not be extended from the port quickly enough. Calais and Dunkirk remain in German hands.

So by this time, it was taking five times the normal fuel load just to perform day to day ops. Thus being "mucked about" is an astonishing understatement at the frustration of such waste of precious fuel. It would seem safe to assume that any entry logs which hinted at such intelligence which could be captured by the enemy would be completely redacted if not physically removed. It was probably never written for these reasons. The explanation is that Operation Market (airbourne attack on the Rhine bridges) started on 17th. Operation Garden was the planned relief of those airbourne forces by 50th (N) Division driving through to Arnhem bridge (the final target) as quickly as possible. Hence the move to a new command and the apparent retreat (to rally and supply, ready for the push) It is almost certain that the company would be unaware of all this at the time of the time.

**September 18th** "Plns with H.Q. in location near BOURG LEOPOLD. Replacement vehicles for those lost in action arriving. Missing TCV turns up ex REME pm – TCVs move out to Bdes and stand by for troop lift into Holland.

Comment: Bourg Leopold (Leopoldburg) is roughly 42 miles East of Antwerp and 55 miles roughly North East of Brussels. It is close to the Dutch Border and the nearest town is Eindhoven (30 miles North North East). It was the launch point of the land troops in the effort to drive the Germans back through Holland. Operation Market Garden was launched on the 17th, they are about to troops to support the paratroops who landed to seize the bridges that would get the British over the Rhine. This battle was noted for "The Bridge Too Far" which refers to the forthcoming inability to reach the paras at the Arnhem bridge which they abandoned on 21st. The rest of the paras near the bridge had to wait until the 25th before they were safely evacuated.

**September 23rd** "Advance continued. 69 Bde runs into trouble and column gets divided. O.C. endeavours contact Plns, but unable get forward. Only information is that vehicles immediately in rear of TCV were badly shot up. H.Q. moved into WAALRE over Dutch frontier. Message from Capt. Hyde with Plns. No casualties. Road between H.Q and Plns cut by enemy."

Comment: It is frustrating that the very historic Battle of Arnhem and the failures to reach the paras at the bridges in time are completely ignored. It seems most likely that they were removed by the censor following the failure at the Battle of Arnhem and the cost of the failure. There is no hint as to where they run into trouble, nor what the damaged vehicles behind their column were carrying, or even belonged to. There is simply no explanation of the blockages that stopped their progress on the roads. It could have been a lack of fuel, or else extremely heavy action and not a word has been recorded over the most intense 5 days of the battle. However, it is historical fact that the planners had overlooked the fact that the road was th only option and therefore, all the Germans had to do was hold it. In fact it became known as "Hell's Highway". It was repeatedly bloked by destroyed vehicles and there was absolutely no other way through. The road was elevated. A large embankment was raised from the notoriously flat surrounds, in order to build a road on top, making it the easiest of targets for the German guns. Every time a truck was knocked out, it created an effective road block for the rest of the column who then became sitting ducks.

Waalre is in outer Eindhoven, about 10 miles SSW of the city centre.

Again, it should be noted that the O.C needs to physically drive to a truck in order to communicate with it. There are no radios. We are so used to mobile technology, "sat nav" and car radios that this hard truth may not be clearly understood.

**September 26th** "Road previously cut now freed, Contact with Capt. H. who states all our vehicles got through before enemy had correct range on road and shelling at our vehicles all fell short - luckily. 1 veh with engine trouble had to be abandoned and was subsequently knocked to bits by enemy. With road open, H.Q. and Workshops move into GEMERT area."

Comment: Gemert is SSW of Nijmegen, about 27 miles by road (there is a dog leg)

**September 27th** "Move for all continued". Tremendous aerial activity. News from 1 Airborne Div not good. Plns cross Waal at NJIMEGEN and push on for ARNHEM. Get some eight to ten miles of it and brought to a halt. H.Q. pulls up on outskirts of NJIMEGAN and gets bombed doing so. Nearly all H.Q. vehicles damaged in this one attack. But only casualty was one man. Few vehicles escaped, but all repairable. Letter received from Brigadier Sir Charles Stanier Bart. Saying of his appreciation and skill of A and B Plns carrying the Bde. Says driving ability , maintenance and camouflage excellent. CRASC confirms and sends congratulatory letter to O.C. A Pln shelled and machine gunned on withdrawing to BOCKE during night. No casualties but some vehicles knocked about. L/Cpl Scott brought in with shell-shock, otherwise everybody cheerful. Colossal artillery barrage all round H.Q for most of night. " Comment: Bocke cannot be identified on modern maps. It was probably a very small hamlet in the region. The severity of the attacks are shown by damage to every single vehicle. It is not clear if L/Cpl Scott is the "only casualty" with shell shock or whether another was physically wounded. It is not clear if the "colossal barrage" is from our guns (which have to have all of their ammunition and food supplies etc. constantly maintained by RASC deliveries) or from enemy fire landing near them. Nevertheless being in range of machine guns is even closer than in range of shell fire. Again, B Platoon are given specific mention (along with A platoon this time). I do know my father, despite his refusal to talk was always very upset about the failure to reach the Arnhem bridge in time to save the attack there. He never mentioned how their valiant efforts were applauded by their own command.

**October 1st** "A & D Plns to NJIMEGEN area 2 kilos from German Border. C Pln continuing maintenance lift. B & D Plns shelled but no casualties other than 2 TCVs, both repairable. Lt. Brooks collapses in road near Bourg Leopold with pneumonia and is run over by passing vehicles."

Nijmegen is 40 miles North East of Eindhoven and within a mile of Germany itself. It is 15 miles south west of Arnhem, which is where the Bridge too far was so nearly captured less than a fortnight earlier. The casual reference to a man collapsing with pneumonia and then being run over by more than one vehicle is again, typical British understatement. No indication of his subsequent injuries from being run over.

**October 2nd** "O.C. visits 24 AEH and sees Lt. Brooks, still unconscious and awaiting evacuation. Lt. Mawer detailed to take over C Pln."

Comment; One has to assume that Lt. Mawer was a second lieutenant already serving with the Company and "acting up" as 1st Lieutenant after the loss of Lt. Brooks. It is (after the last entry) a relief to learn that Lieutenant Brooks actually survived being run over as well as pneumonia.

**October 3rd** "H.Q. digs into NJIMEGEN football ground in middle of artillery. Field mediums and heavy and light ack ack emplacements. Shelling of area with some landing on near vicinity and colossal own replies both with field and ack ack makes rest almost impossible. Fires started by enemy action to N.W. of town. Unit now one officer and thirty other ranks deficient. A, B and D Plns withdrawn to area 7056 Mal-den in order to conserve transport being badly knocked about. Enemy step up shelling of N. from East across location."

Comment: It shows a completely unsatisfactory record that the diary casually refers to the loss of 30 "other ranks" without scrupulously recording when and how these occurred. There has been the occasional reference to one or two losses, but it seems remarkable that this figure has somehow reached 30, without a precise and complete record of these losses. The concern about being in the midst of the artillery only serves to show how perilous it was to be near the artillery. They were an obvious target that was irresistible to the German guns. The mix of medium and heavy gun emplacements in one location (a football ground!) begs lots of questions (one has to assume that the ack ack was to protect the guns from attack by aircraft), but there is no concern about explanation, just with getting away from this sitting duck.

**October 4th** "Enemy shelling of town continued. House on side location gets direct hit, and H.Q. and Workshops personnel do good job rescuing severely wounded civilians. Five in all obtained still alive from debris, due chiefly to work of 20 Coy."

The company diary has made vague reference to civilian casualties, but gives no real sense of understanding. In Normandy, the loss of French Civilians was significantly greater than London suffered throughout the entire Blitz. The Company has witnessed this trail of death for months now. Whilst it is good to read of heroically saving 5 civilians from the debris, one should be asking how many were actually killed by the German shelling of the town.

**October 7th** "Ten O.R's of B Pln wounded by anti-personnel bombs in Malder, all taken to hospital in Nijmegen. Seven evacuated. Two very seriously wounded. Two vehicles damaged and fourteen tyres rendered u/s. Capt. Hyde and O.C. visit hospital. Place crowded and men lying on floor of church. Where conscious, our wounded all cheerful and tough."

The loss of 10 injured from one platoon is the worst recorded in the whole log, but there is no explanation as to what they were doing, nor how many came to be wounded. It is the most detailed log of damage and casualties in the entire log and seems to mark a notable change of style. It seems probable that a different person has taken over responsibility for diary entries.
**October 9th** "Coy on maintenance lifts under 30 Corps. C Pln off road for 48 hours. H.Q. moves to Grave mid-day. Enemy shell location just left with very heavy barrage and shells land in among old H.Q. lines."
Comment: The phrase "maintenance lifts" (whereas previous entries had simply said "maintenance") clarifies the entry. It is not the vehicles being maintained, but ferrying men and supplies to and from the front lines. This was the day to day duty of the Company when it was not transporting troops on a "push". Locations are no longer in all caps, but normal print. Grave is about 7 south west of Nijmegen town centre. It is clear how lucky the H.Q were to have dropped back in the nick of time. It also implies how badly Nijmegen was being hammered by German guns. There is no hint as to why C Company is off the road for two whole days. It seems highly plausible that this may have been due to damage from shell fire.
**October 12th** "H.M. the King inspects Guards A.D. at Grave barracks and passes through H.Q. location. Nijmegen again heavily shelled"
 There could be a hint of frustration here that the King (laudably close to heavy fire) should inspect the Guards, but "pass through" the men who were transporting and supplying them (without noticing).
**October 16th** "Lt. Braund returns to unit vice Lt. Brooks."
Comment: This is unclear. There has been no previous reference specific to Lt. Braund and I cannot make sense of the use of the word "vice". I infer that Lt. Braund has returned to the Company (from some point previously) to take the place of Lt. Brooks who has been sent home and will be unfit for duty for the duration, in which case Lt. Mawer would return to his previous duties within the Company.

**October 18th** "Coy goes out comd 30 Corps and comes under 12 Corps.
Coy to come under 12 Corps Troops – cancelled to come under CRASC 53 Div. TCV to proceed on maintenance thence concentrate for Troop lift and to rendezvous five miles north of Nijmegen."
Comment: It is clear that confusion has returned and that contradictory orders are paying no regard to the RASC men. The final order suggests a push to Arnhem as the rendezvous is just 10 miles short of the town.
**October 19th** "Troop lift completed 3.0 am Shelling of road in VEHHEL area causes traffic accident in which Capt. Adams has severe knock on nose."
Comment: This is intriguing. In a civilian road accident, a "severe knock on nose" would indicate possible head trauma, as the impact was clearly "severe".
Nevertheless, it seems to be passed off as a humorous incident of little concern. It does however show the risk is constant and injury is not restricted to direct hits from gunfire.
**October 20th** "Coy comes under comd S. & T. 12 Corps."
Comment: without further research, this merely seems to indicate the carelessness with which the Company is passed from command to command without receiving clear purpose.
**October 21st** " Coy moves as a Coy to Eindhoven area. Maintenance duties commenced."
Comment: Falling back to Eindhoven (away from constant threat of gunfire, allows the Company to undertake its regular ferrying of men and supplies at less immediate risk to its vehicles.

**October 24th** "TCVs on Troop lift immediately on conclusion long maintenance job. 11.10 pm. 90 TCVs sent where 34 required. Speed at which they reached their rendezvous was considered to be main factor of night's attack. Capt. Hyde at head of vehicles reached RV with break-neck speed and then spent the whole night in a search for "someone who knew anything about our being wanted." Coy comes under CRASC 15 (Scottish) Div who issued streams of duplicate orders. At 4.30 pm. 15 TCV returned to unit lines at same time as signal arrived instructing them to return. Personnel unfed and unrested in 48 hours, most of which was utterly unnecessary."
Comment: The frustration of a lack of co-ordination a waste of men and precious fuel and a futile sense of being passed backwards and forwards is tangible here. The "streams of duplicate orders "shows a clear breakdown in communications and scant regard for the tactical and strategic importance of making best use of a scarce and vital resource. The lack of care for the men is spelt out clearly in the final sentence.
**October 25th** "Vehs. Returned 2.15 and instructed to concentrate for yet another detail. Detail received for lift of Sups 2.0 pm."
Comment: It is unclear what "Sups" are, but it probably means "supplies" (as opposed to Troops). There is a clear point made again about starting one operation immediately after completing another without food, rest or respite.
**October 26th** "Urgent request for every vehicle to be off road for 48 hours to DDST 12 Corps granted. Hence the slogan "the wheel that does the squeaking is the one that gets the grease.""
Comment: The O.C. has finally stepped in and drawn attention to the situation and earned the Company a very long-overdue 48 hour respite.
October 28th "Unit carries 15 (Scottish) Div into TILBURG. No casualties."
Comment: Tilburg is 21 miles North West of Eindhoven (well inland, away from the border). The "No casualties hints that this was far from safe.

October 30th "Unit comes out of comd and goes under comd 8 Corps".

Comment: Given previous example of the frustration and regularity of such changes, one can only take this as further frustration and confusion. The following completely abdicates from the diary format, but is reproduced verbatim from the Company diary" It is largely descriptive text and self-evident. There is little need for further comment.

"With failure of Arnhem as a place of passage, the whole company, under 8 Corps arrangements went on to maintenance lifts or refuges details. Throughout the months of November and December , Platoons worked long and arduous hours helping the build up of big supply dumps and at the same time moved many thousands of Dutch refugees from areas close the battle line. At time of off-duty it becomes possible to organise dances and visits to varying entertainments in Eindhoven, meanwhile all ranks were comfortably billeted and well-liked by the local citizens. Apart from one or two incidents such as the disappearance of some seventeen hundred bottles of beer at conclusion of a beer lift, which caused some officers headaches and the O.C. no little anxiety and a night in a wood, the daily round continued somewhat monotonously.

A party given by the Company to the children of Aalst was a tremendous success and resulted in an illuminated address being presented to the unit with a letter as under:

Aalst, N. Br. Holland

10 December 1944.

To All Officers, N.C.Os, and Men or:
20 Coy R.A.S.C. (Troop Carrying.)
Dears Sirs,

The party to which you invited our children on St. Nicholas Eve was so wonderful, and they enjoyed themselves so very much, that we were several days, looking for a way to show our gratitude. For it was marvellous. They haven't had a better party for many years.

Finally it was impossible for us to give each soldier a souvenir in separate form. Therefore we hope you will take this letter with all our signatures, as a demonstration of our thankfulness.

We give you the assurance that we shall never forget all you did for us and our children.

Before you came here we knew that you would be our friends, but we never had the idea that the friendship should be so very large.

Our best wishes to you all in these difficult days and the future.

LONG LIVE OUR LIBERATORS
SIGNED: F.VISSER
SIGNED: MAGNIN

Then follows signatures of the Parents of the children who attended the party..

Just as arrangements for a Christmas altogether were being made, orders were received to move forthwith to BUDEL, on the Belgium-Dutch border. Coy moved into new location and again commenced making arrangements for Christmas, when a move for all Platoons to lift 43 Div. in the Sittard area came through, and as is now a result of Runstedt's push through the Ardennes. H.Q. stayed put, and nothing more exciting happened then for no accountable reason, Workshops set themselves on fire and a Court of Inquiry came along concerning the disappearance earlier on of 1500 wireless sets from the dump in OUJK. From all these enquiries 20 Troop H.Q. got nearer to the East bank of the MAAS, then winter descended. Severe frosts and snow in abundance make transport details extremely difficult and great credit is due to all drivers for keeping vehicle grief down to an absolute minimum and much less than most companies. Acknowledgements must here be made to Capt. Deck and his Workshop team for maintaining the availability and getting new engines into vehicles under weather conditions so severe, that it was quite impossible for a man to work for more than a few minutes at a time without his hands becoming numbed if not frozen.

Came the New Year and ….

**1945** Diary Continued:"

**January 1st** "Considerable number of enemy aircraft operating over company area and machine gunning. Platoons with 130 and 214 Brigades and standing by to move."

Comment: The lack of a Christmas for the men is clear and on New Year's Day, it is business as usual. Further reference would be required to explain any significance regarding 130 and 214 Brigades. Here, it just seems like another day and another delivery to be made.

**January 2nd** "Platoons engaged carrying working parties for digging of defences in AACHEN area."

Comment: Aachen is in Germany. It is 64 miles south east of Eindhoven, but only just over the German-Dutch border. Aachen was first taken by the US 1st Army in late October. It was not of military importance, but was the capital of Charlemagne's First Reich and therefore psychologically significant. The first Army replaced its losses with raw recruits and the Germans quickly exploited this. It took support from the more seasoned US 9th Army in the South to restore a hold on the city. However, the Germans launched the Winter offensive (the Battle of the Bulge) and threatened to over flood the area (by control of the nearby dams). This offensive started on December 16th in the Ardennes (many miles south, in Belgium) but was a massive threat to the invasion collapsing. Hence, there was no time for Christmas, even north of the German push. As the lack of supplies remained the major threat to the advance, the RASC had clearly had to support the US Armies, whose own transport corps estimated that they were at least 50% under-strength due to the lack of ports. Again, this shows how crucial the precious resources of fuel, trucks and drivers were to the entire invasion forces.

**January 9th** "Same detail continued. Severe wintry conditions show no sign of abating."

Comment: Severe wintry conditions would severely hamper "digging in". This work has presumably been happening every day for a week by now. As the first city in Germany to fall, it was seen as vital not to be thrown back across the border.

**January 10th** "Platoons proceed carry Brigades into the line and return with elements of 52 Div. finally concentrating in the MECHLIN area west of MAAS."
Comment: Maasmechelen (North of Maastricht) is 35 miles North West of Aachen

**January 11th** "Unit carries out a supply detail and then rejoins 130 Bde for troop lift.
Comment: The Battle of the Bulge is still precariously balanced. It would go on for another 2 weeks. It is an extremely dangerous time with a serious threat of Allied forces being overrun. (Hitler was promising another Dunkirk)

**January 14th** "Part Coy. Troop lifting. H.Q. moves back across MAAS into NEERHAREN. All details being affected by icy conditions and difficulty of maintenance of bridges across MAAS. Drivers as a result having long and cold hours on vehicles. Every detail completed in all instances. Unit under comd 12 Corps and carrying out supply lifts up to Jan 20th."
Comment: Neerharen is 5 miles south of Maasmecehelen (and 4.6 miles north of Maastricht). The British Army has clearly been sucked south in order to support the beleaguered Americans.

**January 21ST** "Lt. Lambert and 22 TCV of A Pln carrying 7th Hampshires shelled in area SH.3.7767. and 8563. No casualties but leaguering area for all in midst of own medium artillery and O.C. as result of visit concerned that only short time will elapse before enemy artillery puts over pin-pointed reprisal barrage. Move for TCV comes before enemy reply and guns pull out. No casualties.

Comment: This is the very first time in the diary that the number of TCVs is mentioned. From this, I infer than each of the 4 platoons in the company has 25 TCVs, Thus 100 would be full company strength; this would leave 4 platoon commanders, HQ and Workshop staff adding to the 100 drivers. This is purely guesswork, but a reasonable one, given the lack of any concrete information. The precariousness of the company's safety is clear. It seems the O.C. is not convinced by the impression of his superiors that there is some protection from being placed in the midst of artillery. The O.C. has been proved right already at Nijmegen.

**January 22nd - 26th** "Supply details for all available task vehicles less 22 of A Pln"

Comment: A Platoon is presumably still with the 7th Hampshires, but there is no indication as to where they are. Although the entry is mundane, maintaining delivery of supplies and troops during the final days of a pivotal battle can hardly have been as mundane for the men as the entry suggests.

**January 27th** "42 TCVs join 22 TCV of A Pln for lift of 214 and 129 Bdes in area 7868."

Comment: detail of how many TCV's are involved is both interesting and informative. Sadly, there is no indication as to how the 43 was made up by the remaining 3 platoons. It is also frustrating that the detail of the map reference is lost due to the lack of the corresponding map.

**January 28th** "Capt. Hyde transferred with view to transfer to Infantry. O.C. puts in strong protest without result. Troop lifting continued. "

Comment: It is intriguing how this has come about. There is no indication as to whether or not this was at Captain Hyde's request. From earlier entries, it has become clear that Captain Hyde is pivotal to the company. He would have been directly over the 4 Platoon commanders (all Lieutenants), but unclear as to the hierarchy above him.

**January 30th** "Good news. Coy to move as a company to EINDHOVEN. Popular with everyone, except those with admirers in Reckem. Capt. Hyde returned to unit having been able to convince authorities of RASC requiring him. Advance party proceeds to EINDHOVEN and commence billeting. Thaw begins and roads start breaking up. "
Comment: Reckem is a tiny village near Neerharen. There appears to have been some fraternisation with people of the opposite sex, which has never been entered in the diary before this. The move back North to Eindhoven follows the successful defeat of the German offensive. It does not mention what a close thing this was, merely metions that the thaw is setting in (The damage would most likely due to the pressure of heavy traffic, including tanks over the weeks prior to the thaw).
**Feb 1st** "93 TCV operating under 43 Div arrangements."
**Feb 2nd** "H.Q. to EINDHOVEN and workshops to AALST, O i/c Workshops having bulshed O.C. into believing no accommodation available near H.Q. Workshops therefore back in old billets and laughing."
Comment: this is the first time I have ever seen the word "bulshed". It is clearly army slang for "bullshitted" which in itself is a recently acquired phrase from the Americans. It may be an historic sign of the decline of our language due to the unfortunate mingling with people who had strangled our language into one of their own. Otherwise, it is quite light hearted.
**Fed 3rd – 9th** "Troop lifting of 43 and 53 Divs in areas LIERRE, TURNHOUT and NJIMEGEN. Workshops hard put to provide demands made on them for Tpt, but succeeding by long hours and hard work."
Comment: Lierre possibly refers to Lier (Belgium has 2 different languages, so place name vary). Lier is 18 miles south east of Antwerp. It is 52 miles west south west of Eindhoven, whereas Turnout is 30 miles from Eindhoven on the same road. Nijmegen is 50 miles north north east of Eindhoven, so the company is spread over a wide circle. This shows the daily miles being covered routinely. There is clearly pressure on the Workshops to sustain all the vehicles through such heavy demands.

**Feb 13th** "Big push to SE of Nijmegen. 60 TCV go forward with ammunition and then commence an ammunition flog right up to the guns in CLEEVES." Comment: Cleves is Kleve in German (although after they shifted Anne briefly on to Henry Viii, Cleves seems to have stuck). It is 16 miles east of Njimegen, (thus a journey from Eindhoven of about 60 miles). Again, the number of TCVs is not broken down by platoon. It is not clear how far the guns (at Kleve) are from the front line, but the push into Germany is clearly re-established after the Battle of the Bulge. The following is taken verbatim from the diary, which has abandoned the normal style of entry once more:

" The rest of February was spent in building up supplies in the area beyond the Maas just over the German border and ferrying troops in and out of the line while the area between the Maas and the Rhine was being cleared.

H.Q. was based throughout in Eindhoven, which if inconvenient at times, had compensation features, in that when duties permitted a return to H.Q. , the amenities of Eindhoven and comfortable billets were immediately available. Meanwhile Coy came under command 27 Tpt Coln and the Dutch civilians suddenly found all manner of merchandise returning to them ex places such as Cleeve, Gelden and Goch. Bicycle and big stuff floggers were pursued, but all got away with it!

Leave allocations to the U.K. were very disappointing and strong representations were preferred to 1st Canadian Army, being being now under 1st Canadian Army Command. Came March and the build-up continuing until March 11th , when units went under 30 Corps command – nearly moved on March 12th, but didn't, and came under comd 46 Tpt Coln then at Gemert. Signs of a big push coming were now apparent, and on 13th March unit carried 53 Welsh Div out of battle to Brussels returning on 15th to carry 2nd Army rear forward in to Horst area. The weather now had turned really good, and on 23rd March unit to0k 53 (W) Div to Kevelaer back in Germany."

Comment: I infer that the reference to 27 Tpt Coln may mean what is now the 27th regiment of the Royal Logistic Corps and Coln may means Koln (Cologne in English). There seems to be a blind eye to looting in Kleve, Gelden and Goch (German border towns) and selling these goods on the black market to Dutch civilians.

The gist of the leave issue is that the Canadians had command of the company at the time and ignored strong representations for some leave for the men. Instead, what leave allocation was available all went to the Canadians.

Gemert is 25 miles north east of Eindhoven. Kevelaer is a cross the border in Germany. Horst is 24 miles east of Eindhoven, just inside the Dutch border with Germany.

**March 25th** " 94 TCV Leaguering in WEMB area with 53 Div. H.Q. and Workshops now moved into area close behind, and under comd CRASC 53 Div."

WEMB was a district about 4 miles further north from Kevelaer centre. Wemb is now Weeze airport.

**March 26th** "20 Coy across Rhine, carrying 53 (W) Div. Enemy attack on bridge (unsuccessful) occurred as B Pln were in act of crossing. No casualties."

Comment: travelling in the enemy homeland is met with increased desperation. Soldiers are no longer fighting for the Reich, the Nazis or the Fuhrer, they are defending their homes.

**March 27th** "Plns push on to Vissel with H.Q. and Workshops close behind in Rear Div area."

Comment: Vissel is 13 miles North East of Kevelaer

**March 28th – 29th** "Push continued through to Bocholt and beyond. All German towns badly smashed, dead lying about in dozens and fires burning days after Plns get by."

Comment: Bocholt is 20 miles further north east It is about 50 miles East (as the crow flies) from Nijmegen. The fires burning days after shows that the Platoon subsequently goes back and forth with troops and supplies, rather than continuously pushing into Germany.

**March 30th** "H.Q. and Workshops into Bocholt. Big fires 11 burning. Capt. Hyde and 48 TCV back to Rhine for lift of 156 Bde of 52 Div. Lr. Crowther and 38 TCV goes forward with 158 Bde 53 Div, with rear doors off and mortars mounted in Drivers cabs. Dvr Medley shot through leg, otherwise no casualties.

Even by the time H/Q. catches up with the drive through Bocholt, 11 serious fires are burning. It has been mentioned how battered other German towns have been en route. The scene seems to be one of total devastation. It is known how the German civilians suffered during these last days of war. I do not know the significance of "doors" off, but the measure of mortars set up in the cabs, in the passenger seat area is alarming and extreme. One wonders if it is intended to provide a barrage as the vehicles speed past the enemy. The wounding of Driver Medley may be due to intensive fire on the columns. There is no indication either way.

**March 31st** "Plns through to Winterswijk and Rede. H.Q to Bocholt, Town badly damaged. Streets littered with dead and many fires burning."

Comment: This is the last piece of diary available. Winterwijke is 14 miles north east of Bocholt.

It is frustrating not to know what happened next. What is known is that the Company took part in the relief of Belsen. Bergen-Belsen is 210 miles from Bocholt and the camp was relieved on 15th April. After 4 German fighters attacked the camp on 20th (5 days after it had been surrendered unopposed) destroying vital water tanks (Typhus was endemic and thousands were dying), a 4 week operation took part to move people from the infected camp to a former Panzer Barracks nearby. This was designated Bergen-Belsen DP (Displaced Persons). In those 4 weeks, 29,000 people were moved. Most of them extremely weak, many of them stretcher cases and transport was the only way they could move. There is no indication how fast 20 Coy reached the scene, nor how many other companies were involved, but moving 8000 people per week was a phenomenal exercise and would have been very demanding. It was certainly traumatic. My father never forgave Germans for the horrors that he saw (and would never speak of himself). It left him indelibly marked by the sheer horror of the place.

The Germans did not surrender until May. Berlin surrendered to the Russians on May 2nd. It was not until the 4th that the Germans surrendered North West Germany, Denmark and Holland to Montgomery. Thus the 210 mile trip to Belsen was entirely through Germany which was still at war, with troops defending their homeland. Even Holland where they had crossed the border in March was still defended by German forces until the 4th May. There is no record of how that trip was made, nor what they experienced as they went 210 miles in a matter of weeks, whereas it took them months of hard fighting to get through Holland. There is enough to say that it was ruin, devastation, and resistance that they encountered in Germany. Although free passage into the camps was given to the relieving forces in April, German fighters were still attacking the camp a week later. It is unthinkable that the Company were allowed free passage over that incredible rush of 210 miles unless it was after the surrender on 4th May. That would leave them less than 2 weeks to help the evacuation which ended on 18th May. Whichever the case, it was a horrific way to end a journey full of fear, pain, death and dreadful privation and which was inadequate preparation for their first two weeks of peace time, after 6 whole years of war.

It is perhaps unsurprising that the final chapter of the Company's front line experience was not recorded in the Company diary, or perhaps it was simply something the owner did not wish to preserve. Either way, it is frustrating not to have a record of the final chapter in the remarkable story of a ride.

## Chapter 3 Operation Pluto

It is known that the Company was instrumental in Operation Pluto. This was based on the Isle of Wight and involved building and laying a Pipeline Under the Ocean. It was, of course top secret and little was known of it before a film (by Midland Bank) was made in 1994. Even then, it remains little known in itself.
Pluto stretched to Britol and to South Wales for trials originally, and then was laid across the channel to give security of Oil supplies to the invading forces. Until this diary was found, my brother and I both believed that the 20th Company RASC had worked on this throughout the war, that my father served in Britain and saw no action. After all, PLUTO was fully operated by the Royal Army Service Corps, who had also been instrumental in its construction.
There are sites which tell a little of the project. Wikipedia for example relates the invention, the trials and the laying of the cable, except of course it doesn't. There is detail about the engineering, testing, cable-laying at sea and technology involved.
It utterly ignores the work that was required and carried out on land. Hence, "Operation Pluto" remains pretty meaningless in terms of the RASC who were solely responsible for operating it, right up until the end of the war (and beyond). It is a clear case of the more you learn, the less you know.
Visually, it may be a huge disappointment to visit the remains of the pipeline in Shanklin (by the Post Office). Furthermore, once expects such a vital secret to be protected from sabotage. The impression now given is that it simply lay openly across the land from Shanklin , then under the Solent to (presumably) somewhere in Hampshire and then across to Bristol and South Wales. I am certain this isn't the case, but it is not even considered by those writing about Pluto.

There is no explanation of what the RASC di in terms of laying the pipe, managing the logistics of maintenance and supply. There is no explanation of the land-based operation at all, but I do know my dad spent a long time there working daily on this operation with a hell of a lot of others whose part is almost totally forgotten now.
It is known how the board of the Anglo Iranian Oil company approached Mountbatten (as Chief of Combined Ops) in 1942 and trials began soon after.. Technical stuff including engineering and maritime laying are explained in some detail. Yet whole chunks of its history are now evaporated. I cannot tell you who was involved from when, where they lived and what they did. I cannot even tell you for how long. Luckily, Operation Pluto was just a bit part in my dad's story, yet given how dear it was to his heart, it is almost totally gone. As would have been the following scraps of information had no one bothered to record them.
We have no record of how long my dad was actually involved there, not when he started nor when he left. He certainly had fond memories of his time there and later went to several mini-reunions on the Isle of Wight. I even remember one holiday there myself, but could only have been about 5 or 6. He went back many more times. Somehow, after we learned of Operation Pluto, we built a picture of this is what my dad did in the war. Turns out we were very wrong. This was just one of the things my dad did in the war and much as he loved the Isle of Wight, he did do a bit of travelling.

## Chapter 4 V bombs

Very few British will have any inkling what this has to do with Holland. The image we have in our heads is that these weapons were all fired at London. In actual fact, the majority of these weapons were not fired hopefully towards London, but were a desperate bid to stem the allied invasion. V2 rockets were even fired on Germany itself, Remagen received 11 attacks. The world's first supersonic missile was being aimed very deliberately at my dad and his mates in an effort to stop their progress, all the way through Belgium, Holland and Germany itself, despite being a long way from London.

We talk of Remembrance, but it is startling how little we knew in the first place. Inevitably, that has faded and distorted over time, and these days, all we recall of the V2 was that the people who designed and built them were expunged from all blame for the thousands of deaths of the slaves who built these things under appalling conditions. After all, if you can help the Yanks beat the Russkies into space (they didn't), what's a few tens of thousands deaths?

In just a few months after D-Day the RAF lost over 17,000 men over France, Belgium and Holland. Again that is a largely unknown fact. We think of the raids on Germany as the be-all and end-all of Bomber command. In fact the urgency to destroy V bomb launch sites was vital to the invasion and effectively all raids over Germany were suspended until this was achieved. From the death rate, you get an idea of how hard this proved to be.

The V1 was known to Brits (who did not actually exist until the Internet) as the "Doodlebug". It was the world's very first cruise missile and it was scarily effective. In fact, just think how you would feel if you were being attacked by cruise missiles (against which you feel virtually indefensible). Now imagine that in in a world that had never seen anything like it before. London was defended by a ring of anti-aircraft guns, radar tracking stations, and specialist fighter aircraft. Those chasing the German Army were not blessed by such luxury. The problem was those pesky Germans kept moving, obliging the Allies to follow suit, whereas London tended to stay in one place and was therefore easier to defend.

The V2 was the world's first ballistic missile. It travelled 4 times the speed of sound. The first thing any target knew about it was when it hit. It was undetectable and unstoppable and therefore terrifying. The first ever attack was fired from Den Haag (the Hague) in Holland. It hit Croyden, killing two, but bringing new terror. 3,172 were fired. 2,754 were killed by them in Britain, but few people understand that that was less than a third of their total death rate. Over 9,000 were killed by V2s (surprisingly few, an average of about 3 people for each (very expensive) rocket). However, the received wisdom that London was the target does an injustice to the bravery of others. 1,402 V2's hit Britain, 1,358 hit London, next highest was Norwich which was hit by 43.

In contrast Belgium was most severely hit. Liege received the same total as London itself. Antwerp was even worse, being hit 1,610 times. Hasselt, Tournai, Mons and Diest were also hit many times. France got off relatively lightly; Lille was hit 25 times; Paris 22; Tourouring (very near Belgian border) 19, Arras 6 and Cambrai 4. These were being sprayed at the advancing Allies, not random cities. It was a constant and terrifying threat and the top priority of the advancing troops was to locate launch sites and put the out of action. In fact, in March 45, Hitler ordered 11 V2 to be fired at his own people in Remagen, Germany to destroy the bridge over the Rhine. He killed more of his own civilian people there than the 6 US army casualties. Yet we still think it is all about London and those brave cockney sparrers who won the war single-handedly. I do not mock their suffering and gallantry, just the absurd notions that we have grown up with about the Second World War.
V1 attacks were far more prolific and until October 1944 when the last launch site in firing range of Britain was overrun, a daily average of 100 V1s were fired at Britain. After that however (contrary to our ignorant perceptions) they were not finished. 2,448 V1s were fired at Antwerp after that date (and of course, more were fired at surrounding areas).
I find it frightening how little of this is known. How little understanding we have of the terrible suffering of the Low Countries in the Second World War. We hear loads about the French Resistance, but nothing about the Dutch. Perhaps we are led by this carelessness to imagine the Dutch did not resist. They did, and they died very bravely. The reason it is not told is because of the total success of the Germans in infiltrating the Dutch Resistance network and doing immense damage to the Allies by successfully turning that network and securing a way of feeding us false intelligence. It is likely that a turned Dutch agent betrayed Operation Market Garden before it even started. Thus, the very brave civilians who fought and suffered are expunged rather than admit an embarrassment to the British.

Few people know that the Germans blockaded Western Holland, causing famine which killed over 22,000 people. 4.5 million Dutch civilians were starved during this famine. To illustrate the devastating effects of such experience, we can use on example (because she was later famous). Audrey Hepburn spent her childhood in the Netherlands during the famine. She had lifelong negative health effects of being in that famine. She suffered from anaemia, respiratory illnesses, and œdema throughout her life. Luckily, she had a bit more dosh than your average victim to help with her medical care.

We talk about Remembrance, yet largely we don't have the first inkling of the suffering, cruelty, privation, terror and heroism that went on. It is embarrassing how glib we have become about "Remembrance"

## Chapter 5 Operation Market Garden

When I was a kid, I was fascinated by a brass model my dad had of Nijmegen Bridge. When I asked if it this was "the Bridge Too Far", he simply said "no". I never questioned it again. I was puzzled at how upset my dad was about this episode of the war. I suppose I put it down to Regimental pride. The RASC were there of course, they were after all everywhere (despite the nickname Run Away, Someone's Coming). There had clearly been a terrible failure and I inferred from my dad's evident discomfort that he felt a sort of guilt about it. I put it down to anger at the sense of futility as well as the expense of failure. It was both costly and demoralising nationally.

The received wisdom is that the Paratroops did amazing things and were utterly let down by the failure to relieve them at Arnhem. All of that is absolutely true. What is absolutely wrong is the implied assumption that it was the fault of the troops in Operation Garden (Market was the Airbourne assault, Garden was the relief of the attackers). I never really took much notice beyond this facile perception, but then I had never understood that my dad was right there at the front of this sad debacle. Bitter Paras complained when they were eventually recued "where were you?. Surprisingly, some of the relieving troops were less abashed than you might imagine. They responded "We've been here since before Dunkirk. Where have you been?" These men had fought their way home through Dunkirk and then gone on to fight the North African Campaign, which was at that time the single British success. They were given no respite on D-Day, not just because they were experienced at fighting, but mainly because they were the only British troops experienced in winning. Their infamous 18 hour delay after taking Nijmegen Bridge was not the "gutlessness" of the men, but the incremental decision-making of their leaders.

At this point, the 50th (Northumberland) Division were the very spearhead of the race to Arnhem, but the bigger picture of XXX Corps gives a far better idea of the scale of this operation. On 17th September in preparation of the arrival of the airborne attack, 300 guns of the Corps Artillery opened fire, to soften up the enemy prior to the attack. That is a lot of guns, a lot of men and an endless shuttle of munitions trucks to keep them firing. Tanks and infantry of the Irish Guards (all part of XXX Corps) led the advance and 60 years later, I still believed my dad was on the Isle of Wight rather than in the thick of all of this.

General Horrocks, commander of the XXX Cops believed the advance to Eindhoven would take two to three hours. After all, it was only 13 miles. However, they only managed 7 miles on Hell's Highway after being ambushed by infantry and anti-tank guns dug-in on both sides of the raised embankment which made the road such a death trap. Fierce fighting was necessary to clear this opposition. One single gap took 12 hours to construct a 190' Bailey bridge over a stream at Valkenswaard. The planners had simply not factored in how exposed the single road was. The enforced delay in getting towards to the airbourne troops was not the fault of the poor buggers who found themselves in this hell. It is also shameful how little is known about their heroic battle and their terrible situation.

It is not widely understood that XXX Corps troops were instrumental in taking Nijmegen bridge (in conjunction with the paras). The bridge was supposed to have been taken before they arrived. Yet again, they had to fight for it when they got there. The boats they needed to achieve this were not there. The wait for them was nothing but pure frustration to the troops who were desperate to press on. It is tragic that the delays were blamed on them. The planned support was to have been from a glider infantry brigade, who weren't even able to leave England because of bad weather (for flying). Thus the planned resource simply never arrived.

After they had taken the bridge at Nijmegen, the Guards Armoured Division were all over the place. The Coldstream Guards were fighting in Groesbeck, The Irish were defending an attack back in Eindhoven, The Grenadiers helped take the bridge and got 5 tanks across it. The Welsh Guards were in reserve with the 82$^{nd}$ airbourne. Thus the Guards Armoured division were spread over a 25 square mile area aroundthe south bank of the river Waal. Horrocks ordered them to re-group and this prevented those 5 tanks from charging towards Arnhem. It is highly unlikely that 5 tanks would have arrived there had they simply sped on, but that is conveniently forgotten by the bitter recriminations of a planners cock-up.

Having no plan B against a scenario where the only possible route was one single, highly exposed road. It was not only vital for advance, but the only means of supply. It was so easy to defend. Either side of the embankment, land was very marshy. It was impassable to vehicles. Every time the Germans knocked out a tank or a truck, they stopped the whole column because they had blocked the only way to Arnhem. The road from Nijmegen became, not only extremely exposed (and dangerous), but a very long traffic jam. My dad was in the middle of it and I never knew until long after he died.

In fact, XXX Corps continued to fight all the way, but were forced to do so and that added to the delays. On 25th September, the 50th (Northumberland) Division (with whom my dad was driving a troop carrying lorry) arrived at the front and attacked the Germans holding the highway and didn't manage to take it until the next day. Operation Market Garden was a huge affair. The Allies committed 35,000 troops to one of the biggest assault landings ever made. It was not the fault of XXX Corps that bridges were not taken as planned, forcing them to help take them and slowing them down. It was not XXX Corps fault that bad weather forced them to hold back and do the job of soldiers stranded in England. It was not the fault of XXX Corps that planners made ludicrous oversights and failed to have any contingency plans. It was not the fault of XXX Corps that they did not get through on time, yet they took the blame from people ever ready to make simplistic assumptions in order to distract from their own short-comings.

**Chapter 6 The Battle of the Bulge**

Almost everyone knows about the Battle of the Bulge. (perhaps "Battle of the Ardennes" was a less catchy name after the debacle of losing France and the Low Countries in 1940). It was a film celebrating good old Uncle Sam beating the odds. Hollywood has a long, sad history of doing that. However, such propaganda does permeate through. My impressions were that the Yanks got sucker punched, but by sheer weight of numbers finally managed to stall Hitler's last throw of the dice. I did find it risible that, having lost the country through the absurd idea that the forest of Ardennes was impassable, they allowed it to happen again, but I did believe it had nothing to do with the British. Nothing seemed to have sunk in and the idiots let the Germans do it for a second time. Perhaps it was easier to accept if we put it down to Uncle Sam bumbling along like he had in the death throes of World War One. Unbelievable, but partially true.

The Bulge was the huge inroad the Germans managed to make in the Allied Lines by, once again, bursting through the Ardennes forest. The plan was to divide the Allies (Monty's British and Canadian army to the north and Omar Bradley's $12^{th}$ American army to the south), but far more importantly, to take Antwerp.

It is worth outlining basic logistics to show how crucial this was. After D-day, all the reinforcements and supplies (food, ammunition, petrol, medical supplies etc.) had to be shipped in from Britain. 2 Mulberry harbours had been built, but one was wiped out in a storm almost immediately. The other was badly damaged, but the repaired Mulberry was the only way of bringing everything needed by all of the Allied armies ashore. This created a huge bottleneck as these supplies had to then be delivered to the front, which was spread over hundreds of miles. Having blown up the railway network to disrupt German supplies during the Normandy invasions, trucks were the only option available. The only way was by lorry. The Americans created the "Red Ball Express" (they would!). Essentially motorways were redesignated as one-way roads allowing 12,500 tons of supplies to be moved out of port every single day. Even so, they reckoned they need twice as many trucks to meet the growing demand. By their own estimation, without a deep-sea port, they could not supply the drive all the way into Germany. By taking Antwerp the Germans could stop the invasion.
Securing Antwerp was vital, it was the only deep-water port that would allow supplies to be delivered nearer to the advancing troops and would remove the precarious bottleneck of supplies. More could be shipped in (and out) far more efficiently and quickly. More importantly, without a deep water port, the US estimated that they were only capable of equipping 50% of their needs. However, the Germans seemed somewhat reluctant to give it up and thus Allied supply lines were stretched and vulnerable.

Fuel was a real problem. By now, thanks to Pluto, getting Fuel to France was not a problem. Getting it to the front from the coast was quite another matter. There were no truck stops, not even a petrol station along the way. The trucks had to carry their own fuel. A British 3 ton Scammel (basic British transport) could carry 500 x 5 gallon Jerry cans. However, it would need to deduct its own fuel requirement for the full return trip before off-loading the remainder. As the front line advanced, supply lines got longer. By the time the front was at the Belgian-German border, trucks used 5 times more fuel than they delivered. Tanks are very greedy beasts and tend to sulk without gallons of fuel to guzzle. Thus, the further they drove inland, the more precarious became the supply lines.

For that reason, the Allies suspended all major offensives in October, simply in order to improve the supply situation (allow stuff to be moved inland without it being instantly depleted by immediate use). Market Garden had actually succeeded in some ambitions and had stretched the front line even further inland and across a wider area, thus stretching supply lines even further. Had the advance continued, the danger of having those supply lines grew incrementally. The use of Antwerp would greatly relieve that pressure and alleviate the risk, but it was unknown how long the Germans could and would hold out there. George Patton was infamous for his gung-ho attitude and a forward charge would leave him perilously exposed as it became more and more difficult to keep his army supplied. They had an unfortunate habit of using both fuel and ammunition at an industrial rate. The Germans had experienced this many times with their Blitzkrieg.

The decision to stop the rapid advance and strengthen supply lines was a timely one. It also presented an opportunity for counter strike and Hitler (whose fortunes had serially faded) badly needed to repeat the audacious, so he decided to repeat the format that had initially brought him astonishing success. Taking Antwerp could have been a reversal of the D-Day successes. It could turn the tide once more. So the Germans burst through the Ardennes once again. Taking the allies by surprise, however, they were aware that they only had half the fuel they needed to reach Antwerp. It was vital therefore to raid and capture Allied fuel dumps on their way. As usual, the blitzkrieg approach brought startling success. The Allies were taken completely off guard (which was careless, to say the least) and the German advance was rapid (as usual). The charge was led by the infamous Joachim Pieper. At the start, he had 4,800 men and 600 vehicles. It seemed like 1940 all over again as the allies crumbled in their wake and fled back towards the coast.

This explains one of the biggest puzzles in the Company War diary. The chronological entry day by day falls apart in October and there is no dated entry between) October 26th and January 1st 1945. The explanation turns out that they were a bit busy. On top of that, at some point they seem to be absorbed into the American army, which struck me as a bit odd. Truck drivers in the American army were invariably negroes (over 75% of the 6000 vehicles on the Red Ball Express were negroes). My dad and his mates clearly weren't, so one has to presume it was a conscious decision rather than a mistake.

It turns out that Monty himself made that decision. He had been vying with Bradley for priority of supply and eventually Eisenhower resolved the bickering by taking the US 1st and (the Armies out of the command of Bradley and put them under Monty. That is how my dad joined the yanks and explains where he got his lifelong fascination with and love of all things American. (War does funny things to you).

The pieces have only recently fitted together, after years of reading, researching, pondering and head-scratching. In the company war diary, everything is very confused between October 44 and January 45. It now makes sense. The diary clearly refers to the time spent consolidating the supply lines (establishing and supplying supply dumps along the delivery route to reduce delivery times, and also spread the storage across many sites rather than have all the eggs in one basket. Then, suddenly sometime around Christmas they are rudely uprooted in some hurry. I now understand that this was to move the anti-tank unit which they had just been assigned to dig-in with others of XXX Corps along the Meuse to halt the German advance. In fact they were the only tactical reserve available and the situation was desperate, hence the need to drag them out of their R&R and rush them to the front line. Not only did dad miss Christmas that year, but there was a crippling cold snap which made conditions extremely harsh.

Basically, XXX Corps saved the day. The breakthrough had taken everyone by surprise and the German advance was frighteningly quick. The 101st Airborne looked lost when they were invited to surrender by a surrounding German Army (bringing the incredible, if apparently forlorn response by way of the one word response- "Nuts"). The situation was desperate and all hinged on Patton's ability to liberate Bastogne. The British 3rd Tank Regiment (taking advantage of the improvement in weather) finally stopped Pieper's advance. Of an original force of 4,800 men and at the onset, 800 men managed to escape on foot abandoning the last 100 of an original 600 Vehicles. Pattons's tanks finally got through, relieved the siege of Bastogne and finally liberated the town on 30th. Immediately, they set up the Assensois corridor and a steady stream of Ambulances took the wounded from the liberated city to field hospitals. The Germans used this corridor to launch a counter attack in an attempt to finally take the city for themselves. The counter attack was repelled and XXX Corps then planned their own counter attack. The Gordon Highlanders were to lead the charge (with the Welsh Infantry). My dad had been chilling in Eindhoven with them just before this all kicked off and now he would take them on the offence. They were invisible because they were part of the American 1st Army which ironically was now under British command (they usually leave this bit out).

The battle was America's largest and bloodiest engagement of World War Two. They started with 610,000 men. They lost between 9,000 and 19,000 killed and up to 70,000 to 80,000 wounded or missing. The Germans lost 125,000 men, 67,200 of whom were killed. They never mention how big a part XXX Corps played in "their" victory. In fact no one seems to know they were ever there thanks to Hollywood.

Again, it comes as a shock. Time after time, I have found my dad near the front whereas he always told me he was never there. He is even mentioned (as a driver in Platoon) twice in September for actually fighting to defend themselves after being ambushed. He most definitely told me that he never saw any big fights, yet I have uncovered the Falaise pocket, Antwerp and the V bomb campaign, the Bridge Too Far and now the Battle of the Bulge and my dad was right up there at all of these. Maybe not (in his eyes) doing any actual fighting (He wasn't, after all, deemed fit to serve abroad), but he had actually fought and he was right in the midst of some of the biggest actions of World War Two. I do resent that his medals do not show that he served like this for nearly a whole year, even missing his Christmas dinner in 1944. If his own children didn't even know, how could it ever be remembered? And it is so important that first we understand in order to make sure we properly remember.

It was during this time that atrocities began to mount. On December 17th, Pieper's men notoriously murdered 150 American prisoners, whose bodies were found by US troops ten days later. On 30th, the Germans shot 34 civilians in the village of Bande.  Anger at the callousness and brutality of the Germans naturally spread (No doubt that excuses the murder of 60 German prisoners by US troops at Chenogne on New Year's Day. Whilst Pieper and his men faced trial for war crimes (and many were sentenced to death, including Pieper) the yanks covered their little "tit–for-tat" up and no one was held responsible. Of course such are the victories of war that the winner gets to write the history. Never the less, it shows how very quickly easily people can be goaded into acting like Nazis. Feeling such hatred, they actually felt justified in behaving every bit as badly and just because they won, they got away with murder.

It has taken me years to unravel and make sense of it, but the most intriguing bit of all is still missing. How did he get to Belsen and how long was he there? I know Monty's forces were sent north (so Ike could keep them well away from "winning the war themselves" and the road to Hamburg would have brought them to Belsen, but I do not know where they were on April 15th when the camp was first entered by Allied trucks. Nor do I know how long it took then to reach the camp after 15th, nor how long they were there. But that is typical of dad's war. The drivers were always completely invisible. Indispensable, but so much taken for granted they were never worth writing about from a historian's blinkered viewpoint. Nevertheless, we know he was there and I have a big enough general picture of Belsen to make his story worthwhile.

## Chapter 7  The Belsen Horror Camp.

I do hope you have seen film footage of the relief of Belsen. If not, I urge you do so (YouTube has some clips).It is harrowing but necessary. People must be made to understand as well as to remember. It is easier than ever at the moment to see intolerance to foreigners seems to be ever-growing. Everyone needs to see how this can end. Remember, people were in denial even back then.

For those who like conspiracy theory, Belsen was inadvertently the basis on which Holocaust denial emerged. That was and remains due to ignorance and a lack of understanding of simple facts, yet still it is offered as "proof" that the Holocaust was invented for propaganda reasons and never really happened.

It is inadequate to have a gut rejection of such suggestions. A bit of cold fact goes an awful long way in an argument (even though it is using more and more sparingly these days).

Belsen (which is how it is invariably known) was not a death camp. In fact it looked after its prisoners better than average (for Labour camps, that is not saying very much at all). In fact, initially Belsen was a relatively cushy number. It was essentially established to house "top end" Jewry who had value as barter (forgive the insensitivity, it was theirs not mine).

However, by the time it was relieved, Belsen had become the ultimate horror camp, described by a former prisoner of Auschwitz as the ultimate hell. It is important to explain this, if only to allay arguments against the fallacy of Holocaust denial.

At the time of its relief, press coverage brought challenges and doubts. Much of those doubts were based upon experiences of returning POWs who reported that they had been treated pretty decently. Ignoring the fact that the Wehrmacht and the SS were very, very different organisations, suggesting that a Labour camp was comparable to a POW camp (with Red Cross supervision of adherence to the Geneva Convention) is astonishingly naive.

It is frightening how much we assume. One thing is much like another. German camps, however were never all the same. POW camps were run by the Wehrmacht under the agreements of the Geneva Convention. This included regular inspections, food parcels, correspondence with family at home and most importantly regular food rations and medical care.
Death camps (Auschwitz being the best known now) were simply murder factories. People were literally marched from arrival straight to the showers and were usually dead within 2 hours of arrival. It is generally understood that others were marched away to work (to death), but little else is really understood amongst the general public.
They went in fact to Labour camps. Auschwitz, for example had several camps, not just the death factory. Labour camps were established across the country providing slave labour to massive building and manufacturing projects. These were hideous enough in themselves as people were worked to death, starved, and brutalised, but most prisoners preferred that to immediate death.
 There were other types of camp too. Belsen began as one of those. Himmler designated it a "special camp". It was thus built in March 1943near the town of Hanover in north west Germany to house "Exchange Jews". Bluntly, these were either prominent Jews or Jewish citizens of neutral states who were regarded as possible currency who could be exchanged for German citizens interned abroad. Himmler himself ordered that prisoners (who were, nevertheless, to live and work in very harsh conditions) were to be well treated. This cannot be used to deny the hideous Holocaust and the death factories elsewhere. It is a complete non sequitur to suggest that because Belsen was not a death camp then death camps did not exist.
I will not list the 5 different types of camp at Belsen, but I do urge you to look into that for a fuller understanding. It is not pleasant reading, but not initially as awful as the death camps

A year later, in March 1944, Belsen was redesignated as a "recovery camp" and a further camp was built to "house" women in June 1944. Prisoners were transported from other camps as the Germans looked for more bargaining currency and also to hide the evidence of their crimes. Do not be deceived by the designation "Recovery", no medical treatment was given to assist "recovery". Food was becoming in even less supply and conditions grew more and more awful. The women's camp was occupied by 8,000 women and girls by December 1944. Their conditions were of extreme squalor and there were far more people than there was room for sanitary accommodation.

In January, the vast influx of prisoners brought about further camp redesignations and organization, but conditions continued to decline. By February 1945, there were 22,000 men and women. 7,000 of whom died from starvation and/or disease in that single month. A month later, there were 41,520 men and women, of whom 18,168 died in that month. Nearly all died basically of starvation, despite the fact that there were warehouses full of food just 2 miles from the camp at the nearby army barracks. Reports of cannibalism at the camp begin to spread.

In the first two weeks of April, 9,000 (of the 44,000 inmates) died. They had no capacity to dispose of so many bodies, so they simply allowed corpses to lie where they died and gradually build up into mounds. By April 11th, there were over 10,000 unburied corpses. What sanitary system there was completely collapsed and by now most inmates were suffering from chronic diarrhoea. Other diseases were beginning to arise.

By April 8th, there were 60,000 prisoners in the camp. On that day alone 25-30,000 from other camps arrived (Most were turned away). SS Guards were bringing prisoners from other camps which were about to be overrun by the advancing Russians (in particular). Ironically, the nearby barracks (whose warehouses were stuffed with food) were used as a temporary over-spill.

On 11th April the camp was spotted by an SAS (Phantom) patrol. 7,000 prisoners are sent to Switzerland (One train got through; the other two were liberated by US troops. SS Guards attempt to hide 10,000 unburied corpses.

Hitler ordered the complete annihilation of all prisoners, but Himmler ignored the order (in order to use the prisoners as bargaining currency). Himmler himself ordered the surrender of Belsen, where both typhus and cholera had become epidemic (to put it mildly). Senior officers approach the nearby British under a white flag and negotiate the hand over, warning of the epidemics being out of control, but neglecting to mention the problems of unburied corpses, lack of food and water and sanitation.

A fence was built around a 12 mile circumference of the camp before the first trucks entered on 15th April. It was immediately obvious (after they had absorbed the absolute horror of the place) that they couldn't possibly cope with the scale of the problem. Request for help is met by Royal Army Medical Corps units being immediately despatched and support coming from the Red Cross and the UN (Relief and Rehabilitation Association).

Units arrived on 17th April. On which date a medical conference agrees that the camp has to be cleared. It is given to the 11th Field Ambulance to move the prisoners. This is a unit with 50 vehicles (not all Ambulances). All vehicles were driven and maintained by 80 RASC men attached to the unit which had a total of 200 men. Each Ambulance was permitted to carry no more than 4 patients at a time. Thus it faced 200 round trips per vehicle. Most patients were incapable of walking, so effectively 40,000 stretcher cases demanded more time to load and unload and slower longer journeys.

I am delighted to say that the task of burying the 10,000 corpses was initially given to the SS Guards. Sadly, however logistics soon proved this to be impossible. With Typhus and cholera raging through the camp, dead bodies littered around amongst the faeces and urinary waste of 40, 000 people demanded the swiftest possible clean up. There were simply too many corpses to handle manually (and the health hazard of doing so was immense). Eventually a bulldozer had to be used and pictures of hundreds of naked, emaciated corpses being shoved into mass graves were broadcast around the world.

Incredibly, people started conspiracy theoriesabout such newsreels. They used the fact that Belsen had no crematoria as "prrof" that the holocause was a propaganda lie. They used the experience of returning POWs to suggest that German camps were run humanely. It is truly staggering how many fuckwits there are in this world.

Even with a bulldozer it took well over a week to bury them all. On 20th April, the evacuation was halted because the Germans who were clearing the barracks for reception of prisoners from the camp deliberately sabotaged the water supply.

On 20th April 1575 Platoon of the RASC take responsibility for administration and distribution of food supplies. It is not clear where they have appeared from, but I believe this is where and how my dad got involved. It was an artillery support unit and that is clearly what my dad was involved in until a couple of weeks ago.

It should be pointed out that feeding the starving was medically dangerous and initially a lot of people died from goodwill in that they ate whatever was given them, even though they were too ill to digest such food. Even when nutritionally balanced foodstuffs were developed, inmates could often not eat them. Supplying food was nothing like the picnic it sounds. It was harrowing and shocking and full of frustration. It is hard not to imagine the rage against the Germans for this horror; for their cruel inhumanity, their callous indifference; their pathetic excuses.

From April 21st until May 9th 1,100 people were evacuated each day. Absolutely no mention is made anywhere of the logistics required to feed and clothe these people over that time. All accounts take it utterly for granted. It just happened, but only thanks to blokes like my dad. They don't ever get a thank you, they are invisible.

By 25th April, the daily death rate was reduced to four to five hundred people a day.

On May 4th, further units arrived including 163 Field Ambulance, 2 General (Field) Hospitals (No 9 and 29) Casualty Clearing section and 76 Field Hygiene section (everyone had to be de-loused, bathed and given new clothes) and other Medical units

May 8th was VE day. The Germans had completely surrenders. Three days later the daily death rate at Belsen has fallen to below 100 people dying every single day. Incredible how a horrible statistic sounds like the vast improvement it was.

On 1th May, the excavation is complete. Every inmate has been moved to sanitary accommodation. Two days later, a ceremony is made of burning the last hut. Each hut had been burned after its evacuation because of the endemic disease in the camp. It was the only way to deal with the nightmare.

Between June and September 6th Belsen was used as a displaced persons camp with a largely Jewish population (very much as it was originally designated). It was in the British zone of occupied Germany, it became a self-governing Jewish enclave, By Sept 6th, the last inmates were transported to Palestine for re-settling.

It was about at the point of sabotaging the water supplies that I snapped. I truly wonder how the liberators resisted the urge to murder every one of those vile, unspeakable guards. That feeling is tempered by over 70 years; being spared the first-hand experience: being spared 5 years of fear and death and losing loved ones and rationing; being away from home for months at a time and constantly in danger. How they resisted the urge at the time is truly incredible.

I am delighted that they did not sink to the level of the men they held captive, but intellect 70 years after the event does not explain exactly how they contained themselves. I never understood my father's lifetime hatred of the Germans and everything German. I fought with him for years in my innocent absolute certainty. Once I understood, I am so sorry that I was less understanding (not exactly my fault, as he never said a word about it!).

However, this is a salutary lesson. Just think of the anger these statistics bring out. The unimaginable inhumanity is matched by your instinct for vengeance. There is no such thing as justified hatred, but it is a very human reaction. The Nazis deliberately used hatred to build their Reich. Thank God (whoever that may be) the very natural instinct to respond in kind was avoided.

I would strongly urge everyone to remember this. We can all be turned to hatred. It is painfully simple. It is the easiest way to be manipulated and to be led. For your own survival, I urge you to fight against hatred at every occurrence. Fight racism in particular. I do not mean the pathetic parochialism that white men have used to allow them to pretend to be victims. I mean racism in its only real sense; mindless hatred simply because someone is different. If you succumb to hatred because you allow someone to persuade you that differences are an urgent threat to your existence, then you have become a Nazi. Have no doubt; it can happen to every one of us. There is nothing quite so pernicious as self-righteous indignation. I apologise dad, but I was right, despite the unspeakable things you saw.

As yet, I have no idea how my dad got involved, when exactly he got to the camp, what he did there nor when he left. It brings home how invisible drivers were. Every army driver was in the RASC. The vast majority were assigned to other units (The 11th Light Ambulance had 80 out of 200, but they would all be designated as belonging to that unit rather than as RASC. That is how my dad became a Desert Rat. He was attached to the 50th (Northumberland) as part of XXX Corps. They were bone fide 8th Army veterans from the North African campaign. The RASC identity becomes invisible.

That is why web sites are full of people trying to make sense of their dad's or grandfather's war record. The same questions come up over and over again, because they were never the RASC, they were always some other unit, until recognition was required. Then they simply became invisible.  They were trained to fight as infantry, but were medically unfit to serve abroad. By this time, my dad was 23, but his last 5 years had been in the army. 5 years of loss and hardship and deprivation and danger. Yet, he was invisible. No one even thinks to mention the logistics of delivering food and water and medical supplies to a disaster area with over 40,000 people at a time of war (pretty safe bet that there was not enough supplies within the 12 mile cordon to meet all needs for months). No mention is ever made of the sheer graft involved in meeting this need. Even the Belsen Memorial website gives it no consideration whatsoever.

Every historical account of the war overlooks these details. The logistics are phenomenal; the number of people involved; the extraordinary demands; the number of trips made; even the danger. For example, petrol was delivered in 5 Gallon Jerry cans. The bog standard Scammel 3 tonner could carry 500. Imagine driving that lot under fire!  Or, imagine driving thousands of people who have typhus.

## Chapter 8 Remembrance

For the past few years I have watched as the meaning of Remembrance Day gets diluted and lost. I find it frightening in two ways. First of all, I am incredulous that people have already forgotten and worst of all, I see how easy it is to manipulate the fears and emotions of those who have little understanding. Without doubt, the internet is the main culprit. The quality of journalism has been swept aside by instant news. The quality of that news is barely considered before people react emotionally. Everything is taken as true by the vast majority.

Newspapers like the Sun, despite a hideous track record of malicious lies and immoral methods continue to be cited by millions as if anything in the Sun (or the Mail, or the Express, etc. etc.) is worth trusting. People do not care. They love being instantly outraged. They blindly believe whatever they are told and leap to self-righteous indignation. Understanding has absolutely no place.

These days, poppies appear all year round on web pages demanding "support for our troops". The last Afghanistan war showed how easily the internet is used to mislead people and to get their approval and support.

Remembrance was not originally about "supporting our troops", but in recent years in Britain, the wave of jingoism based on utter ignorance has wiped from the minds of the majority the fact that people from every creed and every corner of the earth were instrumental in defending Britain in the first place and winning the war in the end. These days, it was about 200 Eton boys who spoke dead posh and gave Jerry a bloody nose against all odds. Only Britain suffered (in many minds, only London stood alone).

In the 10 year "War against Terror", British forces lost 450 people, an average of 45 per year. I am certain the allied forces lost more by natural causes during the First World War. There seems to be no appreciation of scale in these days of the internet. The sheer scale of death and loss during two world wars seems beyond modern comprehension, 20,000 British dead in a single day is now subsumed by what the US forces are doing around the world. We know we lost 450 people during Afghanistan, but who knows (or even cares) about the number of dead civilians or even non British combatants? How can we remember when we have forgotten what Remembrance Day is about? It is about the horror, sacrifice and even futility of war. When millions (not tens) of lives have been sacrificed. The idea of Remembrance Day was not only to honour those who have made the ultimate sacrifice but to remind us of the sheer horror of war and use that remembrance to ensure it never happens again.

Sadly, that does not fit with the agenda of Capitalism. The arms trade relies on war for its existence. At over a million dollars a pop for you average missile, it is very lucrative trade. Politicians also find war very handy as a smokescreen against their failures, an instant cessation of all political opposition and a vote-saving tactic. They are easy for big business to manipulate. Remembrance Day can be used to support this Gung-Ho attitude by pretending it is to honour the sacrifices of our current militia. All of whom have chosen their profession and none of whom have been conscripted and sent all over the world without thought for their consent. None of whom are classed as medically unfit to serve abroad. I am not disparaging our troops (nor air force; nor sailors). I am pleading with people to understand a little bit more before we lose it all.

We cannot remember properly if we are not sure of our facts. We need to know our history. I have seen recent posts suggesting that "The Last Kingdom" is a "cheap rip-off" of "Game of Thrones". The former, albeit fictional is heavily based upon the history of Alfred the Great forming the first England, yet the young who see it believe it to be the spin off of some fantasy (involving Dragons). As a lover of history, I know far more about our history than is average. Yet I did not know anything of my dad's war. It has taken a concerted effort to make sense of a "story of a ride" and piece together what it was actually relating. Then it needs setting in the bigger picture and then it brings some understanding and appreciation. This is what remembrance should be about.

No one thinks of the small cogs. Sacrifice meant being wounded or killed and that meant being a fighter yourself. Everyone else was a small bit part. And yet, those soldiers had to be driven to the front and then they had to be supplied constantly with all their needs, including ammunition. Frankly, if I was being shelled or straffed (particularly when sat in front of 3 tons of ammunition) I would rather have a gun than a steering wheel.

## Chapter 9 Conclusion

It was about at the point of the German troops sabotaging the water supplies that I snapped. I truly wonder how the liberators resisted the urge to murder every one of those vile, unspeakable guards. That feeling is tempered by over 70 years; being spared the first-hand experience: being spared 5 years of fear and death and losing loved ones and rationing; being away from home for months at a time and constantly in danger. How they resisted the urge at the time is truly incredible. I am delighted that they did not sink to the level of the men they held captive, but intellect 70 years after the event does not explain exactly how they contained themselves. I never understood my father's lifetime hatred of the Germans and everything German. I fought with him for years in my innocent absolute certainty. Once I understood, I am so sorry that I was less understanding (not exactly my fault, as he never said a word about it!).

However, this is a salutary lesson. Just think of the anger these statistics bring out. The unimaginable inhumanity is matched by your instinct for vengeance. There is no such thing as justified hatred, but it is a very human reaction. The Nazis deliberately used hatred to build their Reich. Thank God (whoever that may be) the very natural instinct to respond in kind was avoided.

I would strongly urge everyone to remember this. We can all be turned to hatred. It is painfully simple. It is the easiest way to be manipulated and to be led. For your own survival, I urge you to fight against hatred at every occurrence. Fight racism in particular. I do not mean the pathetic parochialism that white men have used to allow them to pretend to be victims. I mean racism in its only real sense; mindless hatred simply because someone is different. If you succumb to hatred because you allow someone to persuade you that differences are an urgent threat to your existence, then you have become a Nazi. Have no doubt; it can happen to every one of us. There is nothing quite so pernicious as self-righteous indignation. I apologise dad, but I was right, despite the unspeakable things you saw.

As yet, I have no idea how my dad got involved, when exactly he got to the camp, what he did there nor when he left. It brings home how invisible drivers were. Every army driver was in the RASC. The vast majority were assigned to other units (The 11th Light Ambulance had 80 out of 200, but they would all be designated as belonging to that unit rather than as RASC. That is how my dad became a Desert Rat. He was attached to the 50th (Northumberland) as part of XXX Corps. They were bone fide 8th Army veterans from the North African campaign.  The RASC identity becomes invisible.

That is why web sites are full of people trying to make sense of their dad's or grandfather's war record. The same questions come up over and over again, because they were never the RASC, they were always some other unit, until recognition was required. Then they simply became invisible. They were trained to fight as infantry, but were medically unfit to serve abroad. By this time, my dad was 23, but his last 5 years had been in the army. 5 years of loss and hardship and deprivation and danger. Yet, he was invisible. No one even thinks to mention the logistics of delivering food and water and medical supplies to a disaster area with over 40,000 people at a time of war (pretty safe bet that there was not enough supplies within the 12 mile cordon to meet all needs for months). No mention is ever made of the sheer graft involved in meeting this need. Even the Belsen Memorial website gives it no consideration whatsoever.

Every historical account of the war overlooks these details. The logistics are phenomenal; the number of people involved; the extraordinary demands; the number of trips made; even the danger. For example, petrol was delivered in 5 Gallon Jerry cans. The bog standard Scammel 3 tonner could carry 500. Imagine driving that lot under fire! Or, imagine driving thousands of people who have typhus.

Printed in Great Britain
by Amazon